WIDENING HORIZONS IN
ENGLISH VERSE

WIDENING HORIZONS

in

ENGLISH VERSE

John Holloway

Northwestern University Press

Evanston 1967

First published in the U.S.A., 1967
by Northwestern University Press
Evanston, Illinois 60201

Library of Congress Catalog Card No. 67–12147

Printed in Great Britain

to
GWIN and RUTH KOLB

CONTENTS

PREFACE

THIS small book contains four lectures which I gave in the University of Chicago, when I held the Alexander White Chair there in the spring of 1965. I am happy to recall an enjoyable visit, and record indebtedness to unfailing hosts. The lectures did no more than sketch a large and complex field: many must be better qualified to sketch it than I, though no one adequately. One day, I hope, I shall be able to return to it, and write at greater length; for it is not the concern of literary history in any narrow sense, but (as I argue in the closing pages of this book) helps one to comprehend the general nature of literary culture and literary creativeness, and of their continuance over extended periods of time. In preparing the lectures for publication I have corrected one or two errors and added some notes.

J. H.

Cambridge, August 1965

1. CELTIC, SAXON AND NORSE

*T*o begin this investigation into Widening Horizons in English Verse, let me recall some facts it is easy to overlook. Our own society is so much a forward-looking society, that we are not much concerned with whether our remote ancestors originated in one way or in another. Several centuries ago, English society was static and hieratic, and its members did not look forward to a glorious future of triumph over their environment, as I suppose we do, but they looked backward to their origins; and the legends or the history which seemed to tell them of those origins were of high interest to them. Moreover, in certain respects the people of those times were very ignorant. In the time of Shakespeare and Spenser, which is when my discussion really begins, men had no idea that all the languages of Europe belonged to one large family. They knew nothing about the techniques for assessing the reliability of chronicles and other historical documents. They had virtually no access to any English documents from before medieval times, except the Anglo-Saxon Chronicle. Few could read Anglo-Saxon, and none could read Old Norse. No one in Europe, let alone England, could read the Runic alphabet; and the great early literature of Iceland was unknown even to the Icelanders themselves.

My purpose is now to give a picture, necessarily an incomplete one, of some of the stages by which this ignorance was replaced by knowledge; and more particularly, some of the ways in which this kindled the interest of writers and poets, and entered into their work.

When medieval or sixteenth-century writers thought about the earliest legends relating to England—the native mythology, if you like, of the English people— they did not think about material which was truly English, in the exact sense, at all. They thought about Celtic legends: the achievements of King Arthur—a British king or anyhow not a Saxon one—and of the long dynasty of Arthur's supposed ancestors. This took them back to the mythical leader of the first humans to populate the island of Britain: whose name was Brut. Brut—the connection between his name and the name Britain is obvious—was thought to be one of the nation-founding heroes, like Aeneas for the Romans and Paris for the Franks—who escaped from Troy after the fall of that city as recorded by Homer.

It is a familiar fact, though a remarkable one, that the legendary history belonging to the Celtic peoples of Britain, had come to impose itself on the English, the Anglo-Saxon ones, as well. The chief reason for this was the way in which the 'matter of Britain', as it was called, had entered into every literature of Western Europe during the great period of the medieval

2

Romance. It had done so, as Professor Loomis has argued, largely through the minstrels of Armorica—present-day Brittany—and the accident that the Armorican minstrels were bilingual in their own Celtic language and in French.[1] Besides this is the great fact of one extraordinary book: Geoffrey of Monmouth's early twelfth-century *History of the Kings of Britain*. To say that Geoffrey's standing as a historian is now not high is to speak with moderation. But in spite of the 'old Welsh book' which he declared he worked from, he stands as one of the great mythopoeic writers of Western Europe. Strictly speaking, he did not invent the stories either of Brut, or of Arthur himself. Both these may be found in the ninth-century historian Nennius's *Historia Brittonum*; and the sixth-century writer Gildas refers to battles in about the year 500, culminating in a battle at 'Mount Badon', which was the site also of the last of twelve battles ascribed by Nennius to the 'dux bellorum' Arthur.[2] But the splendid and splendidly entertaining proliferation of the legend is to be found for the first time in Geoffrey of Monmouth's *History*; and he, along with the romances themselves, became the great source for future centuries.

We could take Malory from the fifteenth century, as a writer who took British legend from the French Romances; and Spenser of the sixteenth as a follower of Geoffrey. In Spenser's period the 'matter of Britain' was generally popular with writers, partly because it was looked on favourably by the Welsh Tudor dynasty as meeting the aspirations of the Welsh themselves, and as lending some kind of support to the

3

Tudor's own idiosyncratic claim to the monarchy. Early Arthurian and British legends (or history) are recurrent in the drama of the period, through plays like *Gorboduc* (1562), *The Misfortunes of Arthur* (1587) and *Locrine* (1595), to the pre-Shakespearean version of *King Leir*, Shakespeare's own play, and Beaumont and Fletcher's *Bonduca* of 1614. Spenser set the whole thing out chronicle-wise in *The Faerie Queene*, Book II, canto 10. This catalogue of the early kings of Britain is from one point of view an elegant imitation of the kind of catalogue material which Spenser had found in Homer and Virgil; and it shows how he wanted to invest his poem with the dignity and the temporal range of epic verse at its most ambitious. But it is also a storehouse for us of the 'matter of Britain', more or less as it was familiar in his time. The story of Locrine comes briefly in stanza 14 of the canto, that of Lear and his daughters in stanza 27, Gorboduc in 34, Bonduca in 54. Arthur and his unique position are touched on briefly in stanza 49, and later—since Prince Arthur is of course a major figure throughout the whole of *The Faerie Queene*—Spenser breaks the chronicle of British kings dramatically off, when in stanza 68 he comes to the reign of Arthur's father, Uther Pendragon.

In spite of the skill of this dramatic interruption of the narrative at its point of climax, and Spenser's ingenious resumption of the dynastic and historical story, subsequent to the time of Arthur, in the prophecies of Merlin which come in Book III of the poem, the modern reader does not find this section of *The Faerie Queene*—what shall I say?—irresistibly enthralling. It

4

is less dull, though, when one notices how Spenser worked over his legends, bringing them to life and enriching them for a generation to whom they were of high interest. According to him, the original inhabitants of Britain had been 'hideous giants . . . lurking in loathsome den'; these are the cave-inhabiting giants of Geoffrey's *History*, Book I, chapter 16.[3] But in explaining that Britain was also called *Albion* from the 'white rocks' that lie along its southern coast (these are the chalk cliffs of Kent and Sussex), Spenser was following Camden:[4] he knew the work of the topographers and antiquarians of his time, not only the myth-mongering Geoffrey. In view of this, it is no surprise to find that sometimes he does not take the legendary material very seriously. He is quite willing to add his own inventions to it, in order to work compliments to Raleigh, Sidney and others into the texture of his poem.[5] He is also quite prepared to fuse two of the early legends into one; as he does when he says that the aboriginal giants may possibly be descended from 'Dioclesian's fiftie daughters'. Geoffrey of Monmouth had thought of a good deal, but he seems not to have thought of this.

We can easily trace its origin, though, if we turn elsewhere. Poetically speaking, the culmination of Elizabethan topography was Drayton's *Polyolbion* (1613–22): the 'Many Joys' of the Island of Britain—one 'Song' for each county. Drayton's rich notes to the poem record two early separate legends as to the origin of the giants. The first was that they they were descended from Albion, a daughter of Dioclesian—not the Roman

5

Emperor, but a king of Syria (well, the Roman Emperor of that name conquered Syria: in a field like this, all things hang a little together). The second was that one of the Danaïds, the fifty daughters of King Danaus of Egypt, came to Britain, copulated with spirits, and brought forth a race of giants two hundred years before the time of the coming of Brut.[6] This, one must admit, is jumble and to spare. But what was happening to the 'matter of Britain' in Drayton's time is thrown into relief by the fact that Drayton does not only recount both of these legends; having done so, he *rejects* both.

Drayton in fact is one of the first English poets, if not the first of all, to be interested in material of another kind about the early peoples of Britain. For him the Celts were of interest as a source not of history or legend, but of art. There is a hint of something which links with this in Sidney's famous reference, in his *Apology for Poetry*, to the 'blind crowder' (the minstrel) whose singing of the Otterburn ballad moved Sidney's heart more than the sound of a trumpet. Spenser was hostile to the native Irish as a race, but in his *View of the Present State of Ireland* he shows a genuine awareness of the importance of the bard in the native Irish society even of his own time, and of the high quality of their work as poets and performers of poetry.[7] Drayton, however, was more sympathetic, and therefore perhaps more informed, about the poetic art of the Celts. If I had to choose one writer as marking when a knowledge of non-English and at the same time non-classical culture first truly impinged on English literature and taste, I should choose him.

6

We can tell, from *Polyolbion* Song IV and the notes to it, that Drayton understood the essentially tribal status of the early Welsh bards. He knew that the early Welsh Druids acted as the priests and at the same time the heralds of their people, and (perhaps from Caesar's *Gallic War*, VI, 13), that Britain was the home and centre of Druidic power and Druidic lore. Druids from Gaul came to Britain to learn. He knew of the great early Welsh poets like Taliesin;[8] and as we read what Drayton wrote, we can see his mind coming alive. We can trace, for example, exactly how far his understanding went, in the difficult matter of Welsh metric: exactly how much he understood, and where he began to fail to understand. In fact, of the three main verse forms of early Welsh poetry, Drayton understood fairly well the structure of the two easier forms, but the third was rather beyond him. This was what a writer on the subject has called the intricate and involved ode of the old period. In spite of his limited grasp of its intricate and involved structure, Drayton has something to say about the old Welsh *Ode*; and what he says, though very brief, is also very interesting. Yet he simply says that it is 'of variety in both rime and quantity'.[8] Why is this interesting? Because it enables Drayton to make a certain transition of taste and critical principle, a transition which was crucial to the whole acceptance of verse from non-classical sources.

The principle which Drayton sets up is that in turning to non-classical poetry we are not turning to poetry which defies the canons of the classical. On the contrary, we are turning to what satisfies those canons, and

7

at bottom (though the language may be different and the work may on the surface seem novel and unfamiliar) displays the same virtues and the same kind of achievement. Drayton's account of the most difficult early Welsh form is in essence the same as the account he would have given of the Greek poet Pindar; and in his *Poemes Lyrick and Pastoral* of 1606, we find one ode, that entitled *To Himself and the Harpe*, which makes the equivalence absolutely plain. The harp, Drayton, says, was known in ancient Greece as it was to the Druids; and after praising the achievements of Pindar and Horace, he goes straight on to the bards of Celtic Ireland in his own day:

> The Irish I admire,
> And still cleave to the lyre,
> As our Musick's Mother;
> And think, till I expire,
> Apollo's such another. [8]

Greek, early Welsh, contemporary Irish can all be set side by side and admired for the same reasons. Once the principle was established, there was no limit to the potential widening of the literary horizon.

In the very years when Drayton was putting our poetry into touch with Celtic, others were busily recovering the native Anglo-Saxon traditions. There were several reasons for this. One was that the advance of historical studies, and more generally of a stricter notion of evidence and proof—the whole temper of the seventeenth century as it came in—made men less ready to believe in Brut and Arthur. Drayton felt this movement himself, as we saw. Later in the century, even the University of Oxford was to drop the name of Brut from the list of early kings of Britain printed on the University Calendar.[9] Milton contemplated an epic on some early British topic, but decided that the uncertainty of all such material rendered it unsuitable for a poem of the highest seriousness. On the other hand, several forces had converged to bring the Saxon past into prominence. One had been religious. Archbishop Parker had amassed his superb collection of Anglo-Saxon manuscripts (he left them to Corpus Christi College, Cambridge, where he was Master from 1544); he had arranged for the printing of an Anglo-Saxon sermon and the Saxon gospels; and he had even had a special Anglo-Saxon type cut for work of this kind.[9] All such things, in his view, helped to show, as he put it, 'the antiquity of the thought and customs of the Reformed Church'. Again, the champions of Parliamentary rights against Royal power partly based their claims on the ancient, the Saxon liberties of the English. 'To refer our English laws to [William] the Conqueror [that is, the eleventh century William of Normandy] is a huge Mistake, for they are of far more distant Date', said Selden.[10] There was a special tradition of the ancient love of liberty, and special valour in defending it, among the men of Kent. Drayton mentions the legend that William the Conqueror confirmed the ancient liberties of that county. Moreover, the identification of the Jutes, the original colonizers of Kent, with the Goths, and also with the Geatae mentioned in many early writings, goes back to the fifth-century

9

author Orosius, author of the first universal history treating history specifically as the revelation of God's purposes. This identification was widely accepted. These distinctively Kentish, and therefore Jutish and therefore Gothic qualities, show in Shakespeare's picture of Kent in *Henry VI, Part 2*:

> Sweet is the country, because full of riches;
> The people liberal, valiant, active, wealthy.

The same conception of Jutish Kent as an ancient home of democratic liberty shows in Middleton's *The Roaring Girl*. It does not matter that, as one historian has pointed out, the lawyers who traced common law concepts and Parliamentary rights back to pre-Conquest times were largely in error.[11] That is true enough, because common law emanated from a feudal organization, and the medieval texts showing a continuity back from Norman to Saxon times were apocryphal. But the point is that these Saxon studies came in, in part, for strictly political reasons. 'Gothic' was a Parliamentarian, as 'Gothick' with a *k* was later a Whig taste. On the other hand, the Royalist side looked back to a Celtic past. Percy Enderby's *Cambria Triumphans*, published in the excitement of the Restoration in 1661, reminded the Stuarts of their Welsh ancestry, and argued that 'the manner of Great Britain's government was ever princely'.[12]

Strictly speaking, the literary importance of Saxon studies has been limited. But their importance has been great in one respect: it was with them that scholarship and validly based historical knowledge began to replace legend, as the force widening the horizon of literary taste. We may take, as the starting-point of this process, an interesting little book published in 1605 by Richard Rowland, with the heartening title of *Restitution of Decayed Intelligence* ('intelligence' at this time meant 'information'). Rowland was of Dutch extraction—he had changed his name to Rowland from Verstegen. Perhaps his Dutch origin was behind his wish to replace British myth by genuine Saxon history. At all events, in his work, and for the first time in the field so far as I know, we encounter the mind of a modern historian: sceptical though never scornful of legend, and conscious of how a proper manipulation of the available data can replace it by truth. Thus Rowland saw, in particular, that the place-names of England could be interpreted by means of a knowledge of the Anglo-Saxon language: the fanciful legends which had hitherto been allowed to explain our place-names could simply be set aside. The Humber had nothing to do with the Huns. Rowland was not, of course, the first Anglo-Saxon scholar in our history; but his book marks a definite stage in the progress of Anglo-Saxon scholarship during the seventeenth century. Other landmarks are Sir Henry Spelman's founding of the first Anglo-Saxon lectureship, at Cambridge about 1640,[13] and the subsequent much greater development of the subject at Oxford. This occurred particularly at the Queen's College, where William Nicolson first taught Anglo-Saxon to undergraduates (how often later generations must have lamented what he did!); and at Lincoln, where George Hickes was a tutor.

Hickes was the greatest of seventeenth-century Anglo-Saxonists, and one of the most colourful, as well as most formidable of all English scholars. An extremist Jacobite and non-juror, in 1680 he was deprived of his Deanship at Worcester Cathedral. His response was so intransigent and insolent that he had to go into hiding. Over many years, his finest scholarly work was done while he slipped from one obscure country house to another, dodging his pursuers.[13] His major achievement, the Latin *Thesaurus of the Ancient Northern Tongues*, dated 1703–5, contains not only most notable grammars of Anglo-Saxon, Old Icelandic, Gothic and Old High German, but also, in the *General Preface* and the celebrated *Dissertation*, the first systematic discussions of Anglo-Saxon history, antiquities and law, and the first professional historian's use of Anglo-Saxon charters as basic historical documents.

Volume Three of the *Thesaurus* consisted of a catalogue of all known Anglo-Saxon manuscripts, compiled by the great scholar Humphrey Wanley, Hickes' rival for the headship of Anglo-Saxon studies at this time. Wanley was author of the catalogue of perhaps the greatest of all British literary collections, the Harleian Collection; he was virtual creator of the Society of Antiquaries in about 1707; and in his youth (though described by a contemporary as 'a very loose debauched man') he was Assistant to the Secretary of the Society for the Promotion of Christian Knowledge. His catalogue was a splendid achievement for the time. But even so, it brings out how, from a strictly literary standpoint, Anglo-Saxon studies had a limited importance.

It is clear from Wanley's accounts of both the *Beowulf* manuscript, and the *Exeter Book*, in which are to be found many of the other major Anglo-Saxon poems—'Wanderer' and 'Seafarer' in particular—that he had not read these works, or if he had, was not up to comprehending them properly as poems. Something else also makes clear for us that Anglo-Saxon studies may have contributed indirectly to other and more important literary influences, but had little real influence themselves. This is, the subsequent history of those two manuscripts. The *Beowulf* manuscript was first published in Copenhagen, and even then not until 1815. The *Exeter Book* was not printed until 1842.

To be sure, certain Anglo-Saxon poems were known; and the comments upon them reflect some of the attitudes to Celtic verse which I touched on earlier. John Campbell, writing in the second quarter of the eighteenth century, notes the in effect Pindaric quality of the Anglo-Saxon poet Caedmon: he speaks of the 'furor poeticus' to be found in Caedmon's work. He also makes the claim we met before, with Drayton and the Celtic bards: 'Whatever beauties' he says, 'whatever captivating Figures, whatever Graces of sound or elegances of expression, the Criticks have remarked in any of the Greek and Latin poets, the same are to be found in our Saxon.'[14] But all this was a movement of taste upon a minimum of knowledge. Anglo-Saxon studies were perhaps chiefly of importance as a step towards the ancient literature of Iceland.

. . . .

The idea of Scandinavia—Scanza—as the centre of a major racial diaspora is an old one. It may be found in the *Historia Normannorum* of Dudo of St. Quentin early in the eleventh century. Dudo's very metaphor—'the Danes *swarmed* out of Scanza, like *bees* out of an hive'—was used by Camden late in the sixteenth century, and used again by the Swedish historian Jordanes, chief of the Uppsala circle of Scandinavian historians—one might, I believe, say propagandist-historians—through whose work, as much as anything, Scandinavia came to replace Troy as the great dispersal centre of Europe.[15] It was repeated by James Thomson, author of *The Seasons*, and some while later, reviewing the *Histoire de Danemarck* of Paul Mallet (this book was perhaps the greatest manifesto for northern civilization to appear during the eighteenth century), the historian Gibbon used the metaphor of the swarm once again: writing of the 'essaims nombreux' that issued from the north. Mallet, by the way, was by origin a Swiss, who had become Professor of History at Copenhagen.

The most interesting of these references is undoubtedly Thomson's. It comes in his poem *Liberty*. In this work, the goddess of Liberty describes her own movement through history from one nation to another:

> Thence the loud Baltic passing, black with storm,
> To wintry Scandinavia's utmost bound;
> There I the manly race, the parent-hive
> Of the mix'd kingdoms, form'd into a state
> More regularly free.

(III, ll. 370-374)

Like the Saxons, and like Tacitus's Germans, the Scandinavians stood out as champions and representatives of the spirit of freedom. Mallet makes this very clear.[16] According to him, the early kings of Scandinavia were not monarchs in the autocratic sense: they were the presidents, rather, of a free and self-determining people. In fact, they were themselves elected by that people (one recalls how Hamlet says that Claudius 'popped in betwixt the election and my hopes'); the elections being held in great stone circles like that at Lunen in Scandinavia or near Viborg in Jutland. This is why Dr. Walter Charleton, the friend of Dryden, attributed Stonehenge to the Danes: an attribution upon which, very precipitately we may now say, Dryden wrote him a congratulatory *Epistle*. In 1770 Bishop Percy, editor of the *Reliques of Ancient English Poetry*, published a translation of Mallet's work with the title, *Northern Antiquities*. He noted Mallet's statement that the newly elected king was lifted up on the shoulders of the 'Senators', and he added in a note 'we possess in England to this day a relique of this custom'. What he meant was the custom—now discontinued—of 'chairing the member' on his election to Parliament.[17] I mention these points in order to stress how the movement of literary taste towards the antiquities of the north never lost its political significance.

Iceland, the culmination of this northern achievement from the standpoint of liberty and of literature too, was populated in the ninth century, chiefly by men from Norway who found intolerable the destruction of traditional liberties by the despotic, or if one prefers the energetic, Harald Fairhead. Mallet saw this colonization as the natural development of the traditions of liberty of the Scandinavian peoples. 'The whole settled into form as it were of itself.'[17] (That phrase, by the way, was echoed almost exactly by Wordsworth when he wrote about the popular uprising of the Spanish people against Napoleon—another case of national freedom.) But by the sixteenth century, Iceland had changed greatly for the worse. The incomparable early literature had been almost entirely lost. Its recovery did not begin, inside Iceland, until the seventeenth century,[18] with scholars like Arngrim the Learned or Bishop Bryniolf of Scalholt, who has been called 'the Bishop Parker of Iceland'. On the mainland of northern Europe it began earlier, with Olaf, otherwise Olaus Magnus, Archbishop of Uppsala. Olaus Magnus's *History of the Northern Peoples*, the first notable work of its kind in Europe, was read in an English abridgement to Sir Thomas Browne by his daughter Elizabeth. Browne also mentions, in *Urn Burial*,[19] another masterpiece of northern scholarship, the *Danicorum Monumenta* of Wormius (after whom, by the way—he was a noted physician as well as antiquarian—we name the 'Wormian bones' of the skull). But the astonishing treasures of Old Icelandic poetry were for the most part simply unknown until the chance discovery of the *Codex Regius* on the mainland in 1642. It is this which is now known as the Elder Edda, and which contains the great masterpieces of Old Icelandic poetry.

The scholars of the Scandinavian mainland seem to have been interested in this manuscript, and in other manuscripts coming to light at the time, mainly in the context of one of the major puzzles of seventeenth-century scholarship, the Runic alphabet. Wormius corresponded about runes with the great English anti-quary Sir Henry Spelman; and it was Spelman who first recognized the true ancestry of the word 'rune' itself: that it was cognate with the Anglo-Saxon word 'ryne', a secret, something hidden.[20] Interest in runes may be traced in England, and in English literary figures, throughout the seventeenth and early eighteenth centuries. Browne speaks of them in his Tract or Essay *On Language*. Dryden in his *King Arthur* gives 'runic rhymes' to one character (Celtic or Gothic, it seems to be no great matter), and is aware that runes were used for the writing down of spells and other magical for-mulae. Pope, in *The Temple of Fame*, shows a know-ledge of the legend which attributes the invention of the runic alphabet to Odin.[21] But at the same time, a knowledge of the Icelandic poems themselves was beginning to develop, in spite of their extreme linguistic difficulty.

There is no doubt that one of the most significant figures in the widening horizon of English literary taste is Sir William Temple; and he seems to have been the first to introduce a poem from the Elder Edda to English readers, and to indicate its quality. He does this in his essay *Of Heroic Virtue*, which dates from the mid-1680's. Here, he quotes two stanzas from Wor-mius's Latin translation of the poem now known as the *Krakumál*, but celebrated in the eighteenth century as *The Death Song of Regner Ladbrog*. Regner, a famous

Norse prince or pirate, depending on the point of view, was captured by the King of Northumberland, and thrown into a snake-pit, where he died while composing the poem. Ladbrog, by the way, means Hairy-Pants. 'I am deceived,' writes Temple, 'if in this "sonnet" . . . there be not a vein truly poetical, and in its kind *Pindaric*' (once again, Drayton and his Irish bards come inevitably to mind). 'A . . . rambling sort of wit or invention, loose and flowing,' Temple adds about runic verse in his slightly later essay, *Of Poetry*, 'with little art or confinement to any certain measure or rules; yet some of it wanted not the true spirit of poetry'.[22]

Temple's interest in these matters was doubtless kindled in part by his contacts with the Swedish ambassadors, notably Count Oxenstern (whom he mentions in this context) when on diplomatic mission in the Low Countries. It is rather a pity that he should have quoted from Wormius a stanza in which the Scandinavian scholar had misunderstood his original, and supposed that Regner hoped in the after-life to drink not from drinking-horns, but from the skulls of his enemies. Worse, however, occurred when in 1748 Thomas Warton published two 'runic Odes' based on Temple's Latin, and not only preserved the mistranslation about drinking out of skulls, but also did something unfortunate to the last line of the poem. 'Laejandi skal-ek deyja', this runs. 'Ridens moriar', Wormius put it into Latin. But Warton had 'I smile in the embrace of Death'. The eighteenth century could admire, but not easily imitate, the strength and directness of the Icelandic, and say 'I'll die with a laugh'.

It was Hickes who first printed an Icelandic poem in the original, and translated it.[23] In his *Thesaurus* he included what he called 'The Waking of Angentyr'. In this magnificent poem the maiden Hervor goes at night to the tomb of her dead father Angentyr, and by the aid of spells demands that he rise from the dead and give up to her the sword by which alone she can avenge him. From the tomb, she hears the voice of her father declare that the sword will bring only death to its user. True to the tradition of her race, she is indifferent. At the end of the poem, Angentyr rises from the tomb and yields her the sword. This poem became the Icelandic favourite of the eighteenth century. In 1763 Bishop Percy produced a verse translation of it, along with the translations of four other pieces from the Elder Edda, including the Song of Regner. He also supplied transliterations of the originals, lest he should be taken for another Macpherson fabricating another *Ossian*. Mason in his *Caratacus* of 1759 gave Angentyr's sword, called Tyrfing, to his Romano-British hero, just for good measure: Gray noted this in one of his letters, and referred to the 'confusion between Celtic and Septentrional'. The poem was translated (from Latin, it appears) more than once in the later years of the eighteenth century, and was melodramatized by Matthew ('Monk') Lewis in his *Tales of Wonder*, to the extent that Hervor wins the sword only to find that it gives off flames which burn her up to nothing on the spot. 'He (Lewis) must be a supreme coxcomb on that single testimony,' wrote Anna Seward a little later; she also used the legend, in its unadorned form, in her own verse.[24] It also appeared, needless to say, in the first complete translation of the Elder Edda, that by Amos Cottle in 1797.[25] Southey in his complimentary epistle to Cottle, underlines the 'strong verse' and 'savage wildness' of the older northern poets, and reflects that in the picturesque and wild scenery of Norway, 'the poet's soul / Might best attain full growth'. Set this beside Percy's words—that his runic pieces show 'the workings of the human mind in its almost original state of nature', and one can see several strands of eighteenth-century feeling coming together. One is the growing attraction of early northern verse; another is the general sense of primitive society as essentially poetic, which we can see clearly, for example, in Thomas Blackwell's *Enquiry into the Life and Writings of Homer* (1735); and a third is the primitivism of Wordsworth himself.

It was, however, Gray who made by far the best use, poetically speaking, of what was to be found in the poetry of the North. 'Two pieces of old Norwegian poetry in which there was a wild spirit that struck me,' he wrote in 1767. He gave English renderings of these two pieces—probably he had the help of Latin versions—and they were the *Vegtamskviða*, which he named *The Descent of Odin*, and the *Darraðar-lioð*, which recounts a vision of the Valkyriur, or Norse war-goddesses, supposed to have been seen in Caithness on Christmas Day 1014, the day of the great defeat of the Norsemen at Clontarf outside Dublin. This work he entitled *The Fatal Sisters*. In these two pieces, Gray imbues the conventional eighteenth-century taste for the Gothic and terrifying with a hardness of outline, a terseness of expression, and a vigour of rhythm not wholly unlike his originals and the world from which they came:

> Iron sleet of arrowy shower
> Hurtles in the darkened air.

No smiling in the embraces of eighteenth-century personifications *there*.

Gray's versions from early Welsh are less remarkable, but are part of the same story. In the eighteenth century, the major poets of early Welsh times contributed not a little to English literary taste. To begin with, the political reasons for preferring Saxon over Celtic had passed away. Moreover, Welsh verse was being presented to the English by such scholars as Lewis Morris or his brothers, and Evan Evans: in whose *Dissertatio de Bardis* Gray found the Latin version of Aneurin's early epic poem, the Goddodin, on which he based his English versions. In fact, the Celtic revival was fairly general. *Bonduca* was revived in 1778, and Cowper wrote a poem on the same subject—Boadicea, the chieftainess who led a Romano-British rebellion in the first century AD. Mason's *Caratacus*, as I mentioned before, appeared in 1759. Early Welsh poetry, or at least the glimpses of it which were all the English poet could hope for, fitted in well with the eighteenth-century vogue of the Pindaric, the sublime, and Beauty without Rule. 'Among the bombast of the British and

Irish bards,' wrote Toland the distinguished free-thinker and anti-ecclesiastic of the early eighteenth century, 'there want not infinite instances of the true sublime . . . in stirring up the passions, their elegies or lamentations far exceed those of the Greeks, because they express nature much more naturally.' This is from Toland's *Critical History of the Celtic Religion . . .* of 1726.[26] But Toland did not choose his subject simply from an admiration of bardic verse. Once again, there were political lessons to be learnt as well. The Druids were the ablest of all as a priesthood in producing a religion 'calculated to beget ignorance . . . in the people, no less than to procure power and profit to the priests . . . the history of the Druids is the complete history of priestcraft'.[27]

In some matters, Toland was well-informed. He understood at least the basis of the Ogham script, he could distinguish between Celtic and Norse archae-ological sites in the Highlands, and he may even have seen the stone circle at Callanish in the Hebrides, which is by far the most complete and impressive of all the stone circles in the British Isles, Stonehenge included. If he had not actually seen it, he was familiar with descriptions of it, perhaps those of Edward Lhuyd, whom he mentions, or that published by M. Martin in his *Description of the Western Isles* of 1716.[28] But the equation of Druidism and priestcraft is of special interest in Toland: it clarifies for us the somewhat ambiguous attitude to these matters which is to be found in Blake. Blake knew of the triad, one of the favourite poetic forms in early Welsh verse, and he wrote some examples of this himself in the Preface to the *Descriptive Catalogue*. Sometimes he shows interest in Druidism as an aspect of the patriarchal religion of mankind, and as in fact the source of Greek philosophy (for example, in the Preface to section 52 of *Jerusalem*). But at the same time Blake took Druidism as an early manifestation of the dead and deadening hand of Urizen, and of priestcraft with its repression and terror:

> . . . Albion slept beneath the fatal Tree,
> And the Druids' golden knife
> Rioted in human gore.
>
> (*Jerusalem*, 27)

On the whole, Blake preferred the giants to the Druids:

> The Giants who formed this world into its sensual existence, and now seem to live in it in chains, are in truth the causes of its life and the sources of all activity.
>
> (*The Marriage of Heaven and Hell*)

In the *Descriptive Catalogue,* Blake asserts that the stories of Arthur are merely 'the acts of the giant Albion' [leader, presumably, of the giants who preceded Brut's followers in Britain] 'applied to a prince of the fifth century'.

The main product of Gray's early Welsh interests was of course his Pindaric Ode, *The Bard*. Blake, who knew the poem, saw clearly that there is a fusion in it of 'savage Scandinavian myth' and native British material. In fact, there are also plain echoes in this poem of Pindar's fourth Pythian Ode. But the well-known refrain:

> Weave the warp, and weave the woof

which has no ancestry in Celtic myth, comes from the Norse poem which Gray translated as *The Fatal Sisters*. As for the situation depicted in the poem, Gray probably found the (apocryphal) account of Edward I's massacre of the Welsh bards in Carte's *History of England,* published in three volumes about 1750; and Carte took the story from a volume of family genealogy in the possession of a friend of Evan Evans. Gray himself obtained confirmation of the story from Evan Evans before writing the poem.[29] Still other strands of feeling and response enter *The Bard* from other sides of Gray's experience or reading:

Youth on the prow and Pleasure at the helm

brings one back to the world of eighteenth-century personifications, though a better one than the embrace of Death we confronted some time ago. A full critical discussion of the poem would be out of place here, but I note in passing that it is this complexity of background, making possible a balance of many different tones, none of them too prominent, which makes the poem a notable success.

No later poet makes such good use of the widening horizon towards the north; and I think this was because of the special quality of Icelandic verse. This verse had easily the most to offer among the corpuses of northern poetry, and the problem of reading it in the original, though hard enough, was less so than with early Welsh. On the other hand, Old Icelandic poetry, in its terseness of expression and hardness of feeling, offered something which was simply too remote from the sensibility of the nineteenth century. Gothic horror, the cult of the sublime, and perhaps also something aristocratic in the traditions of the time of Gray, gave a man of Gray's powers at least a chance, though a slender one, to make some kind of genuine contact with Icelandic.

Consider for a moment Matthew Arnold's poem, *Balder Dead,* written largely in 1854. It is based on a translation of the Old Norse *Gylfaginning,* of which versions were published by G. W. Dasent in 1843, and by I. A. Blackwell in 1849.[30] Arnold faithfully follows the events of the Norse legend: the blind god Hoder kills Balder by mistake, he does so with the mistletoe spear, the wicked Loki has plotted the whole thing. Arnold also introduces Regner Ladbrog at a dramatic moment in the poem, and all in all he does a good deal to give his piece an authentic northern ring. But his more intimate poetic intentions are wholly at variance with that overt intention. His descriptive similes are Keatsian:

> Hoder touched his arm.
> And as a spray of honeysuckle flowers
> Brushes across a tired traveller's face
> Who shuffles through the deep dew-moisten'd dust,
> On a May evening, in the darken'd lanes . . .
>
> (I, 229-33)

and so on. More at the heart of the poem, Balder escapes not unwillingly from something like the 'sick hurry', the 'divided aims' that troubled Arnold himself, and make one think of *The Scholar Gipsy*:

For I am long since weary of your storm
Of carnage, and find, Hermod, in your life
Something too much of war and broils, which make
Life one perpetual fight, a bath of blood.

(III, 503–6)

Finally, when Arnold comes, as of course Gray came,
to fuse the northern with the classical, it is not Pindar
he takes as guide, but perhaps the most poignant, most
melancholy, most romantic *vignette* anywhere in classical literature, the newly dead souls waiting to cross
the Styx:

Women, and infants, and young men who died
To young for fame . . .

It is a celebrated *locus classicus,* beginning its career in the
Odyssey, imitated by Virgil in the fourth *Georgic* and
again in the sixth *Aeneid,* and reappearing in the *Inferno,*
Canto IV.[31] Other parts of *Balder Dead* recall *Dover
Beach.* Arnold could give beautiful expression to his
own range of emotion, but it was a range from which
the *Edda* were remote.

An even clearer example is Tennyson's lyric, 'Home
they brought her warrior dead', one of the lyrics in *The
Princess.* It is very hard not to think that Tennyson's
starting-point for this poem, directly or indirectly, was
a poem in the *Elder Edda* popularly entitled *The First
Lay of Gudrun.* But if that is so, Tennyson transformed
what he found. In the lay, Gudrun is before the dead
body of her husband Sigurd. Her grief is so intense
that she cannot weep. She is like stone. The older
women offer her consolation—of a kind—by recount-

26

ing their own misfortunes and trying to show her that misfortune is simply the lot of mankind. But this is cold comfort. A young woman knows how to bring her relief. She goes forward, pulls back the cloth, and turns the face of the dead man towards his wife. Terribly, but healingly, her grief is unlocked.

Tennyson takes a similar general situation, and he also describes this particular incident. But he rejects it as climax to his poem:

> Yet she neither moved nor wept

he comments. What unlocks grief in his poem is something else, wholly an addition to the original; and it is something which throws into relief a good deal of what was characteristic of his century. His last verse runs:

> Rose a nurse of ninety years,
> Set *his child* upon her knee—
> Like summer tempest came her tears—
> 'Sweet my child, I live for thee.'

Comment is superfluous. But why *summer* tempest? Even here also, Tennyson announces his stellar remoteness from the original. Grief like a winter tempest is something his poem, his poetry, his whole time even, could not accommodate.

We find this same softening of a harsh Norse reality in Morris. Morris, in fact, rendes this very same passage twice over.[32] One account of Gudrun's grief comes in his *Sigurd the Volsung*: an original poem, though one explicitly based throughout on Icelandic and other northern sources:

27

> ... she turned to the King beneath her and raised her
>   hands on high,
> And fell on the body of Sigurd with a great and bitter cry ...
> Long Gudrun lay on Sigurd, and her tears fell fast on the
>   floor,
> As the rain in midmost April when the winter-tide is o'er.

I omit six lines in the middle of this passage: it is suffi-
ciently diluted, and bedizened, without them. Second,
consider the version of *Treg-rof Guðrunar* itself, which
Morris inserted as a supplementary translation into the
Morris and Magnusson prose rendering of the *Volsun-
gasága*. Here Morris cannot well escape something of
the ferocious brevity of the original. But he can escape
a good deal of it:

> Back then sank Gudrun,
> Back on the bolster,
> Loosed was her head-array,
> Red did her cheek grow,
> And the rain-drops ran
> Down over her knees.
> Then wept Gudrun,
> Giuki's daughter,
> So that the tears flowed
> Through the pillow ...

But to my sense, the Icelandic original runs:

> Gudrun fell ... on the pillow. Her hair came down. Her
> cheek flushed. It was drops of rain ran down to her knee ...
> The daughter of Giuki cried till the tears ran into her hair.

The simple fact was, that for all his striving, the
world of the Icelandic saga, and of the Elder Edda, was

too remote from Morris for him to find it. Even as he stretched out, it eluded him. But Morris was not self-conscious enough to have sight, it seems, of this difficulty; and it is just that which marks the difference between his poem *Iceland First Seen*, published in 1891, and W. H. Auden's poem entitled *Journey to Iceland*. Morris writes of lingering a little over the sweetness, and also the travail, of old; but Auden, though he sees the clear parallel between the world of the sagas, and our own, senses that the difficulty of contact remains.

> The lover
> Of islands may see at last,
> *Faintly*, his *limited* hope . . .

but the world of the mainland remains, so like and yet so distant. The tempting identification is just a little too easy. Auden is distrustful. The writer (so the poem ends) runs *howling* to his art. They are howls of self-distrust, I think, and of fear of the unknown, and the delusive as well.

II. ISLAM

*B*etween the impact on English poetry of the world of the north or the Celtic West, and the impact on it of the Middle East—particularly Arabia and Persia—there is a continuity, not a break of continuity. To a quite considerable extent, interest in both grew up not only for somewhat similar reasons, but by the same people. Thus when Henry Spelman founded the first lectureship in Anglo Saxon at Cambridge, as I mentioned last time, it was occupied by Abraham Wheloc, who shortly afterwards was appointed to the first Chair of Arabic at Cambridge—or indeed in the country. Bishop Percy not only edited the *Reliques of Ancient English Poetry* and translated Mallet's *Northern Antiquities,* but also had extremely wide interests in eastern culture. In his essays *On Heroic Virtue,* and *On Poetry,* which again I mentioned last time, Sir William Temple showed equal interest in the north and the east: his underlying interest was to break out, if you like, from the closed circle of the classical. The early French orientalists often had antiquarian, northern-

looking interests too: Galland, for example, first translator of the *Arabian Nights' Tales* into a European language—they made a great sensation at the very beginning
of the eighteenth century; Pétis de la Croix, editortranslator of the *Turkish Tales* (1708) and the *Persian
Tales* (1710); and Baron Caylus, inventor of the halfsatirical *Oriental Tales* of 1743. I mention these French
examples, moreover, since this helps to make clear at
the start another of the main contours of the subject.
Orientalism, later a great Romantic interest, largely became strong in England as a literary and poetic fashion
through the influence of France: a fact which stresses
its own complex part in our literary development, as
well as the complexity of the influence which we underwent from France in the period, say, 1650–1750. This
influence was much more than any narrow neoclassicism. D'Herbelot's great *Oriental Dictionary* of
1697 was used by all the English Orientalists of the
Romantic period, and Beyle's *Universal Dictionary* contains a great wealth of Oriental material presented with
learning and sympathy.

There was one reason in particular why orientalists
were often antiquarian scholars as well. The literary
vision of earlier ages was much inclined to see, between
the peoples of the north or west, and the east, a real and
organic connection. John Twyne, in the sixteenth century, in his work on the early history of Britain, had
rejected the Brut legend (though he retained that of the
giants, led by Albion son of Neptune). But he believed
that the second wave of settlers were the Phoenicians—
an Eastern people, that is, and one to which the early

Celtic peoples, in his view, owed their coracles, magic, style of hut-building, and moustaches.[33] John Speed, in his *History of Great Britain* (1611), asserted that the peoples of *Cambria* (Wales) were descended ultimately from *Gomer,* the eldest son of Japhet. The ark had rested on the mountains of Armenia; later Gomer led his people northward across the plains of Scythia to the *Cimbrica* Chersonesus which was the Latin name for the peninsula of Jutland.[34] Davies, the eighteenth-century antiquarian, had identified Menyw, the first man of the Druidic tradition, with the figure of Manu, the first man, and ancestor of the world, in Hindu myth (Sanskrit Manu actually means man). Pope, in the *Temple of Fame,* suggests that the Druids were, in remote times, the priests of the Scythians. John Pinkerton, in his *Dissertation on the Origin and Progress of the Scythians or Goths* (1787), says that the four original races of Europe were the Celtic, the Iberian (now largely destroyed) the Sarmatians (ancestors of the Slavic peoples) and the Scythians. These last came from Asia and were the ancestors of the Germans and Scandinavians.[35] Such legends are idle but not trivial. Certainly, they point in the direction of some extravagant speculations and guesses; like those of the eccentric General Vallancy, at the end of the eighteenth-century, who supposed that the Hindus had once been in Ireland, that the Irish fairies were of Chaldean origin, and even that the Malay language was full of Sanskrit roots (or rather, for good measure, Sanskrit-Irish ones).[36] Later, there is possibly a link with the conviction of Mr. Hugh Macdiarmid that a great Gaelic-Scythian empire, at a high stage of development, extended from the isle of Lewis to the shores of the Caspian at a time when Athens was uncultivated scrub, and the English, in particular, still lived in trees. But beneath the extravagance, at least in the eighteenth century, there was a genuine enquiry: that for the ultimate origins of the race. As a result, even a scholar of European renown like Sir William Jones notes that the Saxon chronicle —'I believe on very good authority'—brings the first inhabitants of Britain from Armenia, while recent scholars had traced the origin of the Goths or Scythians to Persia; and he even adds that the script of Old Persian has affinities with the runic and Ogham alphabets. (This all comes in the course of his distinguished scholarly work on the affiliations of early languages like Zend or Pahlavi, and the whole Indo-European linguistic complex.)[37] Such a fusion of scholarly research with speculations about ultimate racial origins (of interest perhaps to a psychologist more than anyone else), gives a glimpse of the whole range of impact that orientalism had on our culture.

By the same token, it is important to recognize that interest in oriental did not necessarily conflict with admiration for western classical literature. Most often, it went along with that; a fact which again reveals something of the complexity of taste in the Romantic period, and the clear error of contrasting romantic and classic. This is a major point: three particular examples may make it clear.

First, Collins' *Persian Eclogues* of 1742. In his *Preface* Collins implied that he had translated these from originals given him by 'a merchant . . . who had made it his business to enrich himself with the learning, as well as the silks and carpets, of the Persians'. In fact, of course, the poems are Collins' own. Their model is Theocritus, though it is a Theocritus, as the contemporary critic Langhorne points out in his discussion of Collins' *Eclogues* in 1781, whom Collins clearly knew to have spread his range wider than just the conventionally pastoral and bucolic. If the poems introduce something of the properties, as one might put it, of the Persian world—Hassan with his camels passing 'in silent horror o'er the desart-waste', and the towers of 'Teflis' in 'Georgia's land'—the diction of the poems blends this intimately with a range of response taking us directly back to the *Pastorals* of Pope:

> No more the virgins should delight to rove
> By Sargis' banks or Irwan's shady grove:
> On Tarki's mountain catch the cooling gale,
> Or breathe the sweets of Aly's flow'ry vale.

In these Augustan lines we can see good reason why Collins should have referred in his preface to the elegance of Persian writing, and why Langhorne in his critique should have noted Collins' 'art and address', and his 'propriety'. The influence on Collins from the east was a vague one of subject matter only. His real contact with the poetry of Persia was nil or negligible.

Compare, just over a hundred years later, Arnold's *Sohrab and Rustum*. Arnold provides in his note a passage from Sir John Malcolm's *History of Persia*, but Professor Bonnerot has pointed out that he records a greater indebtedness to a long review-essay by Sainte-Beuve dealing with a translation of the *Livre des Rois,* the *Shah Nameh,* of the great tenth-century Persian poet Firdausi. This translation was published by Jules Mohl during the 1830s, and Arnold made use of many of the passages from Mohl (or from Firdausi, as you like to look at it) quoted by Sainte-Beuve; this does something to bring his poem near to the Persian original.[38] But it is remote from that in two ways. One is that Arnold, as always, used his material to give expression to his own sensibility; and in particular to his unhappy sense of the perplexity and designlessness of life in his own time. Just as the god Balder was something of a Scholar Gipsy avoiding the 'sick hurry' of the battle-obsessed Norse Gods, so the River Oxus with which *Sohrab and Rustum* closes is a 'foiled circuitous wanderer', like the Scholar Gipsy, and perhaps half like Arnold himself. And as Rustum began to realize that he had killed his son—'his soul set to grief, as the vast tide / Of the bright rocking ocean sets to shore / At the full moon'. Again, Arnold touches on the 'tremulous cadence slow', the 'eternal note of sadness' for which the sea is symbolic in *Dover Beach.* Like the pacific Balder, Rustum at the end also repudiates the 'life of blood' and battles of the warrior, and asks for strength to 'endure'. This is not an Eastern epic hero so much as an expression of the poet himself.

More important than this, perhaps, is a fact familiar no doubt to all: the Matthew Arnold in *Sohrab and Rustum* was seeking to put into practice the ideals of his celebrated *1853 Preface.* This meant, to compose a

35

work in which the great action was everything and as such enforced 'the subordinate character of expression'. The poem *Sohrab and Rustum,* following this ideal, naturally turns towards Homer as model, and for this the evidence is profuse. Arnold likens his Tatars to 'long-neck'd cranes' flying south from the Caucasus mountains. This image is taken from a well-known passage in Homer, where the Trojan warriors advancing to battle are likened to a great, noisy flock of cranes. It is one of Homer's celebrated comparisons, and it turns up later in both Virgil and Dante.[39] Rustum aloof and sullen, pitching his tents apart from the main army, is another Achilles. Sohrab's suddenly kneeling before his father Rustum, and grasping his knees, is a neat inversion of the aged Priam's similar sudden movement and action when he goes, in the *Iliad,* to the tent of the hero Achilles to ask for the body of Hector. Rustum's spear-point that

> Blazed bright and baleful, like that autumn star
> The baleful sign of fevers . . .

must certainly be based on Homer's wonderful description of Achilles running across the plain of Troy to his decisive encounter with Hector, and looking like the baleful dog-star of August.[40] I cannot say whether, somewhere in the *Shah Nameh,* the horse of Rustum weeps as it does in Arnold's poem; but the horses of Achilles certainly shed tears at the death of Patroclus.[41] As for the watch-fires that begin to twinkle when evening falls at the end of the poem, they recall one of the most celebrated descriptive passages anywhere in

Homer; that which closes Book VIII of the *Iliad*. If Arnold replaces the dazzling starry heavens of Homer with the 'cold fog' which 'crept from the Oxus' as night fell, that simply brings one back again to the way in which he invested the poem with his own dignified melancholy. Arnold's policy of seeking what he himself called the 'eminent plainness and directness' of Homer through a largely monosyllabic style, one, in this respect, very remote from the Greek original, showed great insight into the nature of English as a language by comparison with Greek; and may, just possibly, reflect his reading of the Norse translations of Dasent. But this matter lies outside my present discussion.

The third work which I have in mind as illustrating how oriental and classical interests could interact and combine lies midway in time between Arnold and Collins. It is a very notable, though now little-read, poem by Walter Savage Landor called *Gebir* (1798). Gebir was considered to be an early Muslim prince of Spain (perhaps there was once, in Egypt, a Hyksos prince Jubair, who founded Alexandria). Legend declared Gebir to have invaded the kingdom of Egypt, and history (it was thought) preserves something connected with his name in the rock of 'Gibraltar'. Landor's enthusiasm for classical authors and classical virtues of style is well known. His participation in the vogue of Orientalism was much more limited, and went in fact with definite opposition to its more extravagant manifestations. His source for his story was a work which belonged to the Orientalist movement (I

37

shall come to it in a minute) but he declared that his telling of the story was entirely independent in all its details. Certainly, there is often a weighty, pithy terseness in *Gebir* which is wholly remote from any idea of Oriental style in vogue at the time, and strongly reminiscent of, for example, Seneca:

> the brave
> When they no longer doubt no longer fear . . .

> One moment yet remains; enough to know
> Soon will my torments, soon will thine, expire . . .

> Compassion can be but where passions are

—these three suffice as examples. There are other signs of classical influence also. The building of Gebir's city in Book II is an echo, in the approved style of classical elegance, of the passage in Virgil's fourth *Georgic*. Milton echoed it also. The snake which is discovered in the process recalls a similar incident in Virgil's second *Aeneid*; the Sixth Book ends with a markedly Homeric description of the sun setting in the sea; and the close of the whole poem is inescapably modelled on the close of the *Aeneid*. Theocritus is also important for the poem. It is not, though, the Theocritus whose mere ghost shows in Pope's *Pastorals*. It is the Theocritus of fresh first-hand description of all the richness of nature; of an almost sinister use of magic and spells, as in the second *Idyll*; and of the later epic idylls which gave little enough to subsequent pastoral traditions.

In spite of all this, though, we have to make an effort to register the exact balance of Landor's poem; and it is an error to see *Gebir* as a classical poem which simply happens to have been written round an originally oriental fable. Coming as it does almost at the height of what has been called the 'oriental renaissance', it is much more deeply impregnated with orientalism than the other poems I mentioned. Thus the journey to the underworld, Book III, mentions 'Erebus' as Homer does, but otherwise has nothing whatever in common with the visit to Hades in the *Odyssey*. Nor has it much in common with Virgil's account of the descent of Aeneas to Hades. There is, however, an inescapable likeness to the 'palace of subterranean fire', and the Halls not of Erebus but Eblis, as these appear in perhaps the chief English orientalizing fable of the eighteenth century: I mean Beckford's *Vathek*, of 1786, only twelve years earlier. In both *Gebir* and *Vathek*, there is a night scene of mountains and a watch-tower, and the earth opens to receive the visitor to Hades. In both, the underworld is something like a subterranean hall of immense dimensions, lit with a dim but irreligious light that is reminiscent of another Oriental fantasy of the period, John Martin's painting entitled 'Belshazzar's Feast'.

Suppose, though, that we put Landor's *Gebir* and Beckford's *Vathek* side by side, and ask what further roots they have in the orientalizing trends of the time. We can soon see that the two works probably point back to two different specific localities in the Near East, two places each of which had outstandingly caught the imagination of the time. The culminating scenes of *Vathek* are set in and near the South East Persian city of Istakr, which was one of the great cities of the Middle East during the time of the Persian Sassanid dynasty in the early centuries of the Christian era, but was sacked by the Arabs in the seventh century, and some time after that fell into total and perpetual ruin. Here it is that the two central characters in Beckford's fantasy descend to the underworld, and explore the 'Halls of the Pre-Adamite Kings': which are undoubtedly related in Beckford's imagination to the superb rock-tombs of Naqsh-e-Rustum, just across the valley from the historical site of Istakr. They constitute, in fact, the tombs of the great Achæmenian monarchs, Darius and Xerxes, 1,000 years before the Sassanids and the heyday of Istakr itself. In *Gebir,* on the other hand, the wicked servant of the queen of Egypt goes out at night to meet the spirit of her dead sister, a sorceress. The meeting takes place in a desert plain surrounded by mountains, amid the ruins of

> Once a fair city . . .
> . . . and with palms refreshed

This reference to the palm-trees suggests what is at the back of Landor's mind as he writes. It does so the more, because the whole meeting is so much like the incident which opens one of the most widely known of all late eighteenth century books: the *Ruins: or Meditations on the Revolutions of Empires,* by Count Volney —published in French in 1791, and immediately translated. Volney's meditations—in sub-philosophy and comparative sub-religion, we could say briefly they were—occur in the ruins of the Hellenic-Syrian city of

Palmyra, celebrated for its colourful splendour, sudden access of power, and disastrous fall, during the third century AD, under the beautiful Queen Zenobia ('she ... equalled in beauty her ancestor Cleopatra, and far surpassed that princess in beauty and valour' wrote Gibbon about her); Palmyra was known also, since the superb illustrated folios of Dawkins and Wood, of 1751, for its extraordinarily fine topographical setting, and Greek-Oriental architecture. The author of the *Ruins* begins his meditations (by moonlight, one need scarcely add) through the help of the *genius loci*: a 'pale apparition' or female spirit which approaches 'through the pillars and ruins of a temple'. Now turn back to the midnight meeting in *Gebir*:

> Before the city she descried
> A female form emerge above the sands

Just as *Vathek* recalls Istakr, so Gebir draws, through Volney, on the contemporary image of Palmyra. Often enough, in this way, poems have their roots in places; places which kindled the imaginations of the writers although they knew of them not through experience, but through the well-known books and the general temper of their time.

But if we trace the ancestry of Gebir backwards a little further, it is another, a pre-romantic world of orientalizing, which comes into view. Landor says himself that he took the story of Gebir and Queen Charoba from a book called *Progress of Romance,* which Miss Clara Reeve published in 1785. Miss Reeve, in her turn, took it from a translation by J. Davies of a French work by Pierre Vattier; which was, in its turn, a translation of the *Egyptian History* of Murtada ibn al Khafif.[42] But Davies and Vattier both belong to the closing decades of the seventeenth century. The earlier seventeenth century, when the chairs of Arabic were founded in Oxford and Cambridge, is the period when relations between England and the Eastern Mediterranean are beginning to take one particular form: trade. This produced not only a desire to have men competent in Arabic, but also the first collections of Arabic manuscripts. In these early times, the Orient has barely begun to interest *poets,* and is the concern of *scholars.* The greatest of English seventeenth century Arabic scholars was undoubtedly Edward Pocock (1604–91), who went as chaplain in 1630 to the English commercial centre at Aleppo and collected a remarkable number of Arabic manuscripts. It was for him that Archbishop Laud founded the Oxford Chair of Arabic, and it was he who translated (into Latin, in 1671: an English version followed several years later) the most interesting Arabic work to appear in this country in the seventeenth century. This was called *Philosophus Autodidactus*—the self taught philosopher— or to give it its Arabic title, the *History of Ibn Yockdan, an Indian Prince.*

The *History of Ibn Yockdan,* originally by a twelfth century Arabic philosopher known to his English translator as Abubecher (really Abu Jaafar ibn Tophail) is one of the last Arabic works to remind us how the earlier interest of the west in oriental writing was for its thought and ideas; as the later was in the first place for its impressions and emotions. This work is the imaginary biography of an individual cast away on an island (one thinks of Defoe, and it is likely that Defoe knew the book); and its purpose is to consider how far an individual can extend his knowledge by his unaided efforts, using the resources of solitary meditation and experiment alone. In view of this, it was of course extremely well adapted to the age of Descartes and Locke. In English, it often reads remarkably like an English translation of Descartes' *Meditations*. It reaches, as the summit of its enquiry, a condition of knowledge which bears a strong resemblance to belief in natural religion, but not revealed. This, once again, is a point of view most consonant with feeling in England early in the eighteenth century—Bishop Butler's *Analogy*, for example, is addressed precisely to those who find themselves in this intellectual position. Last, it rejects over-ambitious and metaphysical investigations, in language which would have appealed strongly to Locke, to Berkeley and their contemporaries: condemning, as the author puts it himself, 'over-curious search, by natural light alone, into such things as neither eye hath seen, nor ear heard, nor are discoverable by the heart of man'.

Turning to the Orient for philosophical, and also for moral and political wisdom, looks back to the period when the Arab world was much more highly developed than Europe in these matters, and was indeed our sole channel of connection with the thought of ancient Greece. The greatest of all sixteenth-century scholars, Joseph Scaliger, had learnt Arabic: the use he had put it to was to translate Arabic proverbs. Pope was acquainted with the *History of Ibn Yockdan,* and mentions it in his *Guardian* essay, No. 61 (May 1713):

> I remember an Arabian author, who has written a treatise to shew how far a man, supposed to have subsisted on a desert island, without any instructions, or so much as the sight of any other man, may by the pure light of nature, attain the knowledge of philosophy and virtue.

The Augustan essayists of the beginning of the eight/ eenth century frequently introduce oriental tales into their papers. But in this period, Oriental narratives were prized for something of a particular kind; a dry pointedness of instruction, that seemed to reside in the exact turn of the story, and was thought to be distinc/ tive of Oriental moral wisdom. Thus Steele, in the *Guardian* 148, says that the *Turkish Tales* of Pétis de la Croix 'happened to lie in my way';—and (he goes on) he 'happened to dip upon' the following short tale. He realizes, amid all these happenings and chancings, that the tale might 'fall into the hands of men of wit and pleasure' who would read it with their usual levity. But he himself tells the story in another spirit: to 'divert and instruct' persons of 'plain and virtuous minds'. It is a tale of the *Santon* (or holy man) *Barsisa,* who lived for a long 100 years in a state of great piety. One day, the king brought his beautiful daughter to him: holi/ ness, it was thought, might succeed where medical science had acknowledged defeat. At this moment the devil puts a wicked thought into the Santon's mind; and now he goes from bad to worse. He keeps the princess in his grotto overnight (no one is suspicious

44

of so venerable—or at least so elderly—a man); he ravishes her and then appeals to the devil; on the devil's advice, he kills the princess to avoid discovery, and offers, when he is discovered all the same, and about to be executed, to worship the powers of evil if the devil will deliver him once again. But by now, of course, the devil has what he wants. His co-operation is abruptly withdrawn.

I have not recounted this fable in order to provide you with a little moral instruction such as Steele had in mind, nor to gratify the levity of men of wit and pleasure: but because the outcome of Steele's telling it was not what he might have predicted or indeed desired. The *Santon Barsisa* is, of course, a brief version—one told for the point not the thrills—of the story which 100 years later was to make up the most celebrated of all 'Gothick' novels: Matthew Lewis's *The Monk*;[43] and if we register the difference between the two texts, we register a good deal of the difference between the two periods, the Augustan and the Romantic. In brief, the composure and succinct wisdom that the periodical essayists found in the Oriental tale was progressively replaced by what Langhorne noted, in his critique of Collins' *Persian Eclogues*: 'all the Eastern poetry . . . is bold, wild and unconnected'; but full nevertheless of 'graceful and magnificent daring'.[44] Sir William Jones well knew, of course, that this was an incomplete account of the nature of eastern poetry. All the same he firmly endorses it as far as it goes. He speaks, in his essay *On the Mystical Poetry of the Persians and Hindus* (1791), of the 'warm imaginations' of the East, and

45

even admits the danger of a poetic style in which the limits between vice and enthusiasm are so minute as to be hardly distinguishable'.[45] In his essay *On the Poetry of the Eastern Nations* of 1772 he had written in a similar vein: 'the Asiatics excel the inhabitants of our colder regions in the liveliness of their fancy and the richness of their inventions'.[46] C. P. Brand, in his valuable book *Italy and the English Romantics* (1957), has pointed out how the vogue of Italian literature was a prominent part of English literary taste at the beginning of the nineteenth century. Italian writing, also, showed richness and lively fancy, and the Italian and the Oriental trends ran to some extent alongside each other. Certainly, one detail which in my own turn, 'happened to lie in my way', affords an illustration of this blending of Italian and Oriental. Leigh Hunt had his oriental interests like others of his period; but in him, certainly, the Italian interest was the primary one. In his *Story of Rimini* of 1816, a poem heavily under an ill-digested Italianate influence, we find a notorious couplet describing the summit of human felicity:

> The two divinest things this world has got:
> A lovely woman and a rural spot.

I agree that this is an idea which might come from life, not books; but I incline to think that Hunt took it, perhaps at second hand, from Jones's essay. 'It is a maxim among (the Arabians)', wrote Jones, 'that the three most charming objects in nature are, a green meadow, a clear rivulet and a beautiful woman; and that the view of these objects at the same time affords the greatest delight imaginable'.[47] The green meadow and the rivulet, at least, must have meant more to the Arab than to Hunt or the Italian characters of his poem; but his using this Arabic conceit in his Italianate poem helps us, I think, to see something of the wider place of orientalism in his period.

Sir William Ouseley, in Volume II of his *Oriental Collections* (1797), comments on the 'wildness and irregularity' and 'rapid succession of extravagant thoughts' to be found in the lyric poetry of the Persians; and attributes it to 'asiatic luxury' in general, and in particular (though not perhaps in justice) to the poets' composing while intoxicated.[48] We can see a comparatively early and moderate example of this rapid succession of thoughts, and a certain wildness and luxury, in the Persian *Song of Hafiz* which Sir William Jones translated in the 1770's, and which I think is the first translation of any Eastern poem into English. Jones preserved the distinctive rhyme-scheme of the original; but in the interests of western decorum he changed the sex of the poet's beloved:

> Sweet maid, if thou wouldst charm my sight
> And bid these arms thy neck infold
> That rosy cheek, that lily hand
> Would give thy poet more delight
> Than all Bocara's vaunted gold,
> Than all the gems of Samarkand.

In the next stanza, however the poet's flower-like Ganymede transpires undisguised:

> Boy, let yon liquid ruby flow
> And bid thy pensive heart be glad

> Whate'er the frowning zealots say:
> Tell them, their Eden cannot show
> A stream so clear as Rocnabad,
> A bow'r so sweet as Mosellay.

The rather distinctive rhyme-scheme, of course, suggested that Persian lyric was not all wildness and luxuriance; and it was not long before this was clearly recognized. J. H. Hindley, in his collection of Persian lyrics of 1800, clearly sees the error of regarding the Odes of Hafiz as 'pearls strung at random'; and well analyses some of the intricate and indeed profound connections of thought which link each stanza with the next. Two years before, Francis Gladwin in his *Dissertation on the Rhetoric, Prosody and Rhyme of the Persians,* published in Calcutta, had fully explained the immense subtlety and intricacy of the Persian poetic. Turn from these works to poems by Shelley like the *Indian Serenade* (pointing, incidentally, toward the Persian culture of North India, not toward Sanskrit) or *From the Arabic: an Imitation,* and one can find in the English poems a number of the devices or turns of expression which conform either exactly or approximately to those elucidated by Gladwin. In all probability, Shelley had no knowledge of Gladwin's book: but he seems to have picked up a good deal from collections of Oriental verse which were appearing in some numbers in the period when he himself was writing.

As for the general influence of the Orient, or rather the idea of the Orient, on poetry in this time, we can take stock of it either in externals, as it were, or more intimately in matters of style. When Byron's *Childe*

48

Harold first lands in Greece, what strikes his imagination is not classical Greece so much as Greece as the Western edge of the Orient: the ferocious despot Ali Pashá in his mountain fortress; the minarets of Tepalen 'glittering' with lanterns for the month of Ramadan; the outlandish soldiers—Moorish, Tatar, Indian—and their colourful wagons and costumes; the Muslim call to prayer sounding from the mosques.[49] But here, the East does not get into Byron's style. Contrast the opening lines of Act II of Shelley's *Prometheus Unbound*. The scene is in what Shelley calls 'The Indian Caucasus', and the spirit called Asia is greeting her sister Panthea. Panthea arrives just at the moment when dawn, with its morning-star in the east, turns into the first hint of sunrise; and it is the sound of Panthea's wings which is referred to at the end of the passage:

> The point of one white star is quivering still
> Deep in the orange light of widening morn
> Beyond the purple mountains: through a chasm
> Of wind-divided mist the darker lake
> Reflects it: now it wanes: it gleams again
> As the waves fade, and as the burning threads
> Of woven cloud unravel in pale air:
> Tis lost! and through yon peaks of cloud-like snow
> The roseate sunlight quivers: hear I not
> The Aeolian music of her sea-green plumes
> Winnowing the crimson dawn?

A style like this—where imagination is all colour and spectacle, a drama of enraptured or nearly over-enraptured senses—may be traced directly back to Sir

William Jones' Oriental translations, and orientalized original poems, published as a volume in 1772. In taking stock of it and its provenance, moreover, we are not simply taking stock of a Shelleyan idiosyncrasy: but of a striking, almost spectacular difference between the second generation of Romantic poets—Shelley, Byron, Keats—on the one hand; and on the other, Wordsworth (and with him Coleridge) whom those later poets in many respects followed, but in this respect broke with completely. Moreover, the influential position of *Gebir* stands out once again, this time in respect to Keats. The inescapable fact that this poem had a great effect on Keats is not a matter only of how the early Keats's fresh, lush descriptions of the natural environment are also in lines of Landor's like:

> How often have I seen her kiss a flower
> And on cool mosses press her glowing cheek.

The inter connections are of situation and story also, not style alone. The whole situation of the shepherd Tamar, at the beginning of *Gebir*, who will 'all relate' to his brother, just as Endymion will to his sister, and who then has an amorous encounter with a nymph who returns next full moon, is pervasively like that at the opening of Keats's poem. Perhaps the influence of *Gebir* was much more widespread in Keats's work. Are, I wonder, Landor's lines:

> the sound
> Of timbrels and of cymbals struck her ear,
> And horns and howlings of wild jubilee

in part the germ of Keats's 'What pipes and timbrels? What wild ecstasy' in the *Ode on a Grecian Urn*? Is the 'palpitating snake' found *'cirque-couchant'* in *Lamia*, an echo of the builders in *Gebir* who turn a stone over and 'see a serpent pant . . . *curling* more close and *crouching* ere he strike'? Even more remarkable is the parallel be-tween Tamar's struggle with the goddess nymph, and the poet's torment-and-ecstasy on the steps of Moneta's temple in *The Fall of Hyperion*.

> Life was almost quivering on my lips

we read in Landor. There is a similar touch-and-go struggle in Keats's poem:

> my iced foot touched
> The lowest stair, and as it touched, life seemed
> To pour in at the toes . . .

More than this, though; not many lines before this struggle in *Gebir* with the goddess we find the following account of Gebir himself awaiting the arrival of the Queen:

> There was a brightening paleness in his face,
> Such as Diana rising o'er the rocks
> Showered on the lonely Latmian . . .

by 'lonely Latmian' Landor must mean Endymion himself. But, the 'brightening paleness' of Gebir's face seems to me also to reappear in *The Fall of Hyperion*:

> Then saw I a wan face
> Not pined by human sorrows, but bright-blanched
> By an immortal sickness which kills not . . .

I should like to be able to consider two other oriental-izing poems of this period: Robert Southey's *Thalaba* (with a Muslim background) and the *Curse of Kehama* (with a Hindu one). These, also, did a great deal to-wards providing the model, in matters both of style and also situation and incident, for several of the more important later Romantic poems: *Endymion*, *Queen Mab*, *Alastor*, the *Masque of Anarchy*, and in some respects *Prometheus Unbound*. Since these two poems, from the first decade of the nineteenth century, in their turn owe a good deal to *Gebir*, and Southey repeatedly stressed his enthusiasm for that poem, the continuity of poetic tradition appears once more; and our picture of the emergence of the luxuriant descriptive style of the later romantic poets grow fuller and more detailed. But it is difficult to set out, in a lecture, the exact textual detail of this kind of continuity, save perhaps as a boring catalogue; and I shall therefore turn to quite another aspect of the Orientalist vogue.

The fact is, that Orientalism had its political signifi-cance just as much as cultivating the Goths, or cultiva-ting King Arthur. On the one hand, the Orient was steadily seen as the home of tyranny on the grand scale. The line is clear from Dryden's *Indian Emperor*, through the 'Persian tyrant' who appears in Akenside's *Pleasures of Imagination* (Book I, line 582), on to Shel-ley's *Ode to Liberty*:

> palace and pyramid,
> Temple and prison, to many a swarming million
> Were, as to mountain-wolves their ragged caves.

Southey is full of this idea, and there is even a hint of it in one of Crabbe's most remarkable though least characteristic poems, *The World of Dreams*; a passage, by the way, in which Crabbe, in his turn, seems to have taken something from *Vathek* and its Halls of Eblis:

> I know not how, but I am brought
>   Into a large and Gothic hall,
> Seated with those I never sought—
>   Kings, Caliphs, Kaisers,—silent all;
> Pale as the dead; enrobed and tall,
>   Majestic, frozen, solemn, still;
> They wake my fears, my wits appal,
>   And with both scorn and terror fill.

But with regard at least to one part of the East, there was quite another attitude. This was the one region of the world which has never, so far as my knowledge extends, been conquered by anyone save its aboriginal inhabitants; and for this reason alone could make a good claim to be the home of human liberty. The region I mean is Arabia Felix, as it was called for so long—Arabia the Happy. In John Dyer's poem, *The Fleece* (1757), there is a picture of the rigours and the poverty of life for the desert Arabs:

> The weary Arabs roam from plain to plain,
> Guiding the languid herd in quest of food;
> And shift their little home's uncertain scene
> With frequent farewell: strangers, pilgrims all,
> As were their fathers. No sweet fall of rain
> May there be heard . . .

> (I, 527ff.)

But Sir William Jones, in his *Poetry of the Eastern Nations*, gives quite another account. 'It is the most perfect of countries ... no nation at this day can vie with the Arabians in the delightfulness of their climate and the simplicity of their manners.'[50] The part of Arabia he has in mind was the true Arabia Felix; the fertile—the *once* fertile—valleys of the Yemen with their spice trees and balsam plants so rich that the air was scented. 'All the perfumes of Arabia' were something that even Lady Macbeth could recall. A country, thought Jones, of fresh streams, vast forests, sun and shade, perpetual spring. But within the idealized notion of the scenery of southern Arabia was another and perhaps more important one: that of the 'simplicity of the manners' of the Arabians. This takes us back to the remarkable account of Arabia by the first European, I believe, to explore its hinterland: Karsten Niebuhr. A native of Holstein in Denmark, Niebuhr began life as a peasant, later acquired some knowledge of mathematics and Arabic, and in 1760 joined, and incidentally was the only survivor from, the expedition to Egypt and Arabia which it is to the eternal honour of the Danish monarchy to have sent out at this early date. His *Beschreibung von Arabien* was published in 1770, and appeared in English at Edinburgh in 1792. 'If any people in the world afford the historian an instance of high antiquity, and of great simplicity of manners, the Arabians surely do. Coming among them, one can hardly help fancying oneself suddenly carried backward to the ages which succeeded immediately after the flood ... Having never been conquered, the Arabian has scarcely known any changes but those produced by the hand of nature.'[51] The Arabian system of government was one of pastoral, patriarchal independence. 'A nation of this character can not readily sink into servile subjection and arbitrary power.'[52] While we ourselves, says Niebuhr, retain only the shadow of liberty, independence and simplicity, and have lost the substance through refinement, the Arab, even in youth, is conscious of his lonely and distinguished situation. He becomes 'pensive and serious even in infancy . . . a stranger to the pretended pleasures which are so eagerly pursued by the youth of Europe'.[53] One cannot but be reminded of the youth described so sympathetically by Gray in the closing stanzas of his *Elegy*. Clearly, the Arab, if he was to be seen in these terms, could serve, rather in contrast to the Persian—or at least the Persian of Islamic times—as a symbol of the more austere and inward side of Romanticism. And when one finds Niebuhr going on to say that in spite of this outward solemnity, the Arabs have 'a great degree of vivacity in their *hearts*',[53] one inevitably thinks of Wordsworth's heart responding to the bliss of solitude, to wanderings lonely as a cloud, and filling at last with pleasure and dancing, as we read it did in *The Daffodils*.

It is no idle association, for we are now in a position to comprehend better one of the most remarkable, and obscure, passages in *The Prelude*: the vision early in Book V of the Arabian with his lance, shell and stone. Later in Book V, Wordsworth records his childhood interest in and love for the 'Arabian Tales' (though in an abridgement). One should bear in mind that the *Arabian Nights' Tales* really belong to, and offer a picture of, not desert Arabia, but the great city cultures of Baghdad on the Euphrates, or Cairo, where the collection seems finally to have been put together. And in *The Prelude*, Book V, it is not the 'promise scarcely earthly' the romance and colour, of the *Arabian Nights' Tales* which is at issue, but the calm, austere picture of Arabian life we have seen in Niebuhr. The Arab, the 'gentle dweller in the Desert' as Wordsworth calls him, is an archetype—I refer by this word to the immemorial antiquity of his surroundings—of the twofold wisdom that men in general can enjoy, and that history (this seems to be Wordsworth's idea) has entrusted over so many ages to the Arabs. The first is geometry in the form of astronomy:

> they held acquaintance with the stars
> And wedded man to man by purest bond
> Of nature, undisturbed by space or time . . .

and the second is poetry, symbolized by the brilliance and mysterious prophetic voice of the shell. The 'calm look' and gentleness of the Arab are strongly reminiscent of the meeting with the pastoral Arab family in Southey's *Thalaba*, Book II. I do not know whether Wordsworth when he described the 'fleet waters of the drowning world', and their glittering light, that pursued the Arab at the end of his 'vision', was taking something from *Thalaba* Book V, where Southey's Arabian youth encountered the 'tumultuous . . . tide' of the underworld; or whether he was perhaps recalling another Orientalized fantasy, *Spectator* paper 159; in which Addison, alleging that he quotes from an Eastern manuscript called *The Visions of Mirza*, describes the huge Valley through which rolls the 'prodigious tide of water' which is part of the great tide of Eternity. But the comparison with Addison is much to the point in any case: for it reminds us of the earlier kind of interest in the Orient, the moral rather than the colourful kind of interest. It is this with which Wordsworth is in contact; and if (as the dates make quite probable) he also borrowed some of the ingredients of his scene from Southey, he invested them with a reserved strange ness, a solemnity, and a reverberating significance, which the slighter poet never attained.

III. INDIA

I mentioned in my last lecture that the seventeenth-century development of interest in Arabic and know-ledge of the Arabic language was partly the result of England's growing trade with the Levant. There is no doubt that a concern for trade, and other practical interests, had a great deal to do with the developing study of Oriental languages almost throughout the period. Long before Napoleon diagnosed us as a nation of shopkeepers, Edward Young, later the author of *Night Thoughts*, had in 1729 composed *Imperium Pelagi* ('Ruling the Waves' one might translate it with the well-known patriotic song in mind): *Imperium Pelagi. A Naval Lyric.* 'Written in Imitation of Pindar's Spirit —and celebrating the signing of the Treaty of Seville.' Its relevance to the present discussion becomes clear from the Preface: 'Trade is a very noble subject in itself, more proper than any for an Englishman.' If today the subject seems a little strange for an essay into the sublime, that strangeness was not felt by Young;

and the poem is a sustained celebration of trade as what its author calls 'the real interest and possible glory' of his country:

> Of human Welfare and Renown
> Trade's the big heart; bright empire, but their eye.

So sure, in fact, is Young of all this, that he goes straight on to describe trade as what built up the power of the two great Empires of the East in his own day: that of the Mogul Emperors in Northern India, and the Tatar Manchu dynasty in China.

After the battle of Plassey in 1759, there was added to the commercial reason for pursuing the study of oriental languages, a political one. England was now committed to a course of constantly expanding political control of the Indian sub-continent, and control of that kind called for more than a knowledge of the appropriate languages. It called for some knowledge of the whole culture and customs of the subject peoples. We can find, in fact, that the repercussions of this on English culture begin to show almost at once. Alexander Dow went out to India in 1760, almost immediately after the decisive battle. He did not return on leave to England until 1769, but he then brought with him his drama *Zingis* (about the great conqueror of that name). It was produced at the Drury Lane theatre, and (though it has no other claim to distinction) has at least the distinction of being the first English dramatic work on an Asiatic subject to be based on first-hand knowledge of that continent.

It was followed shortly afterwards by Eyles Irwin's

Bedukeh, a narrative poem; and in this work one can see very clearly the link between literary effort and comprehending the customs of the new subject peoples, since the poem was a study, and a sympathetic study, of the Hindu custom of Suttee (the suicide of the widow on her husband's funeral pyre). The same principle applies, by the way, to our commercial expansion, at a later date, in China. J. Legge, the first Professor of Chinese at Oxford, stated in his Inaugural Lecture (1876) that the first Englishman to distinguish himself in Chinese studies was the Reverend Robert Morrison. Morrison's initial concern was a religious one: he was one of a notable group of early Protestant missionaries to China. But he had other things in mind besides. Arguing in 1825 for greater study of Chinese, he pointed to both the commercial and the political reasons for it. Our commercial interests in China, he said, were 'enormous'. But what he put first in his argument, even before the missionary need, was the fact that 'politically, the stake of Great Britain in China is not inferior to that of Russia'.

As these principles applied to India in the closing years of the eighteenth century, they bring out a matter of much importance from the literary viewpoint. The clue may be found in Sir William Ouseley's *Prospectus* to the *Oriental Collections* which he edited for a year or so from 1797 on—a venture inspired by emulation, at home, of the series of *Asiatic Researches* which issued from Sir William Jones's Asiatic Society, founded in 1789 in Bengal. Ouseley, like the others, stresses how 'national interests' prescribe the learning of oriental languages. The interests he has particularly in mind are, first, trade, and second, the administration of conquered territories. But although he is speaking of the Indian territories, the languages he has in mind are Arabic and Persian. This is important. Jones in 1783 had been made a Supreme Court judge in Bengal, and had begun an intensive study of Sanskrit in order to master, and indeed to codify, Hindu law. It is plain that this indefatigable polymath aspired to be the Justinian of the Hindus. But it was not any Indian language (strictly speaking) which was the most immediate need of the British in India at this period. It was Persian. Persian was the official, the court language, of the Muslim dynasties of North India, who descended from the non-Hindu, Muslim invaders of the sub-continent from Sultan Mahmud in the early eleventh century onward. Sir William Jones makes clear, in the Preface to his *Persian Grammar,* that all correspondence between the East India Company and the Indian courts was in Persian; and Alexander Dow's *History of Hindustan* (1768) is simply a translation of a Persian work: one written by the sixteenth-century Muslim historian Ferishta. Dow makes the Muslim dominance clear, though in his preliminary *Dissertation* he shows that he has some independent knowledge of Hindu culture itself.[54]

At first, the world of India—its life, its scenery, its mythology and legend—made an impact on English literature which was much like that made by Persia. Or rather, both Indian and Persian cultures were seen, often enough, in a general way as the world of

61

the East, of Islam, without any sharp distinction being made between them. It was reasonable enough, since North India, with its Muslim culture, was both geo-graphically and also intellectually and emotionally more accessible to the European mind. Hazlitt, in his essay, *Why Distant Objects Please*, notices how the imagination endows the distant with the fascination of the exotic. The remoteness of the East, its antiquity, its spectacular objects (juggernauts, poison trees, fearful storms) and its sensuous luxuriance all kindled the imagination of his time, and little distinction was made between the Muslim and any other part of it.[55] Moore's *Lalla Rookh* of 1816, which must now be among the least read of all once celebrated poems, is set geographi-cally in India, but is Muslim throughout in spirit, save where it is Zoroastrian—again, the world not of India, but Persia. *Lalla Rookh* herself is the daughter of the seventeenth-century Mogul Emperor Aurungzebe; and of the tales her future bridegroom tells her in the disguise of a minstrel, the first is set in the time of the Abassid Caliphate (about 800 AD); the second is set in the Muslim Paradise; the third concerns a Persian religious sect; and the fourth is about the favourite of the Mogul Emperor Jahangir, contemporary of James I and grandfather of Aurungzebe. Moore's occasional Hindu touches, like the Mantras (i.e., Hindu reli-gious texts) known by a Muslim enchantress, illus-trate not his ignorance of the distinctions between the two religions, but his indifference to these distinc-tions.

Southey also felt free to take the Hindu world, equally

with that of Islam, as one in which the sensuous luxury and colourful brilliance could freely be found. In his Hindu poem *The Curse of Kehama*, just as much as *Thalaba*, we encounter constantly that sensuous luxuriance of description which I have already discussed. But *Kehama* also shows Southey beginning to make a distinction between Muslim and Hindu. In fact, in his Preface to the poem, he draws attention to that element of the monstrous and grotesque which is rather distinctive of Hindu mythology: 'the religion of the Hindus, which of all false religions is the most monstrous in its fables . . .' (he did not, presumably, mean to imply that the true religion had more monstrous fables still); '. . . no figures can be imagined more anti-picturesque, and less poetical, than the mythological personages of the Brahmins.' Yet for all these words, Southey admits this side of Hindu mythology into his poem, and even makes a good deal of it. There is the 'giant Tree' of Paradise, rooted on a mountain top, with a thousand branches rising into the sky, and a thousand torrents flowing from its base; the fearful dragons, yoked with adamant, of the terrifying Hindu enchantress—herself so different from Moore's enchanting muslim enchantress, who could well have aspired to membership of the illustrious harem she is merely a servant to; then, the chariot of Jaga-naut, with its twenty wheels a side and seven-headed image of the deity; the giant winged horses called Aullays, that have trunks like elephants, and are so big that with these trunks they can throw ordinary elephants about as easily as a sling can throw pebbles. A hundred of these substantial creatures are

63

harnessed to the chariot of Kehama, the vainglorious Rajah, on his journey to conquer the underworld. Here, finally, he and the reader encounter the Rhadamanthine goddess of the Hindu hell, who sits within a cloud from which only her thousand arms emerge as they snatch up the damned.

No harm is done if we speak with a touch of levity of the tremendous and melodramatically awe-inspiring side of Hindu mythology, simply as this is met with in Southey's poem. There is a touch of levity, though to be sure without intention, in the poem itself. Southey was producing, in effect, the nearest that his age could get to the spectacular, superlative-drenched films of today like *Antony and Cleopatra*. Apart from their value as light entertainment (which is not negligible) the value of these poems to ourselves is that Shelley and Keats so much drew on them in making poems of so different an order of seriousness.

But with the original poems of Sir William Jones, it seems to me to be another matter. The poems I have in mind are the *Hymns* to Hindu Deities which Jones composed, for the most part, shortly after his arrival in Bengal; and which were published in the volumes I mentioned just now, the *Asiatic Miscellanies*. Jones stated that some at least of these Hymns were adapted from poems by the great Sanskrit poet Kalidasa, whose play *Sakontala* or *The Fatal Ring* he later also translated. But in effect they are original poems. Shelley must have known them. The metric of Shelley's *Hymn to Intellectual Beauty* is a clear derivation from Jones' *Hymn to Narayena*; and the figure of Love in *Prometheus Unbound* is much more like Camdeo, the Eros of Hinduism, as he appears in Jones's *Hymn*, than it is like anything in Greek mythology.[56]

Speaking generally, one could say that Jones's *Hymns* are in diction not unlike many of the Pindaric odes of the eighteenth century—I have Gray's particularly in mind—but in one respect they are notably different. In brief, this is that they are *philosophical* poems at a radical level. They celebrate the gods as the governing powers of a universe which has a nature and an order. This is particularly true, perhaps, of Jones's *Hymn to Narayena*, the spirit of God as moving on the waters. The poem is a powerful and moving celebration of the creation of the world, and recognition of the continuance of God of whom the created world is a constant joyous embodiment and at the same time a no more than trivial reflection.

There was, however, one Pindaric Ode from the eighteenth century, or a year or so after its close, which could also be called a profound philosophical poem: Wordsworths *Ode on Intimations of Immortality*. I think it very likely that Wordsworth knew this *Hymn* of Jones's, and that it had some influence on him when he was writing his Ode. To begin with, in both poems there is a similarity of rhythm which is by no means the necessary result of writing Pindarics. Both are swift and almost vivacious in their movement. This is because they express much the same feeling for a gaiety, a vibrating vitality and responsiveness in nature everywhere. For both, the world laughs—they use this very word in rather similar contexts—with its own excess of joy.

What

> Glows in the rainbow, sparkles in the stream,
> Smiles in the bud, and glistens in the flower

for Jones—seems much like Wordsworth's sense of things:

> ... the hour
> Of splendor in the grass, of glory in the flower

Both also use very much the same idea of the great ocean of the creation. But what is more remarkable is that for both poets this celebration of the natural world in all its joyous profusion is prelude to something of another order; something in which the sensuous is repudiated, or not far short of that, in favour of the moral and spiritual. The exact emphasis is different in the two poems, but the movement of thought in each is remarkably similar. Jones writes:

> Blue crystal vault, and elemental fires ...
> Mountains whose radiant spires
> Presumptuous rear their summits to the skies
> And blend their emerald hue with sapphire light;
> Smooth meads and lawns, that glow with varying dyes
> Of dew-bespangled leaves and blossoms bright,
>   Hence vanish from my sight;

Now Wordsworth's stanza 10:

> Though nothing can bring back the hour
> Of splendour in the grass, of glory in the flower ...
> What though the radiance which was once so bright
> Be now for ever taken from my sight ...?

I venture to transpose Wordsworth's two couplets, because this brings out inescapably how close Wordsworth is to Jones. The crucial fact is that when the line I quoted just now is looked at in its context, the resemblance does not diminish, it grows. Wordsworth, it will be remembered, finds strength for this situation in 'the philosophic mind' and the faith that looks through death. Jones's *Hymn* ends with the words:

> ... suns and fading worlds I view no more
> God only I perceive, God only I adore.

Speaking more generally of these *Hymns*, sensuous luxuriance of the colourful and extravagant kind goes also in them with an impression of rich darkness, and of the monstrous and grotesque, that shows Jones's full awareness of the great difference between the Hindu and the Muslim theologies, and the extra emotional dimension, as it were, of the Hindu.

The luxuriant, the jungle-like proliferation of the Hindu pantheon was of course no chance fact. It occurred because in the Hindu religion, elaboration of mythology went with, occasioned, and doubtless received support from, elaboration in theology and, most notably of all, metaphysics. The European legend of the East as the home of wisdom could be traced back to the time of Pythagoras or perhaps Homer, and is well illustrated in the anecdote given by Arrian of Alexander the Great's conversation with the Indian gymnosophists.[57] The difference in fact between what Arabia or Persia, and India, had to offer the West, was that the latter, over many centuries, had been one of the two great homes of metaphysics on the planet—Europe, I suppose, being the other. There are brief and superficial references to this, early in the seventeenth century, in *Purchas his Pilgrimage,* the great travel collection; but in English, the earliest systematic discussion of this side of Indian culture seems to come in 1692 in the *Archeologia Philosophiae* of Thomas Burnet, author also of *The Sacred Theory of the Earth*, that late seventeenth-century sport of early seventeenth-century religion, solemnity, eloquence, and prose poetry. Burnet, in his *Appendix*[58] on the Brahmins, shows he is aware that the priestly order of India has Sanskrit as a classical language reserved to it for religious purposes, and also knows that the Brahmin caste had a tradition of philosophical thought over the whole range of the major perennial problems of metaphysics.

Along with this, though at a very different level, one might mention the fact that Indian civilization also had another reputation: that which it partly shared with Persia and indeed the whole East, for serene moral wisdom at the level of the proverb and the terse moral fable. Jones observed that the Greeks called the Indians the wisest of nations, and added 'in moral wisdom they were certainly eminent'.[59] Elsewhere he asserts that the moral fable—like those of Aesop—probably came to Europe from India. He himself translated one of the most famous Sanskrit collections of moral fables, the *Hitopaseda*—which seems to have been one of the planetary classics, if one may so put it; I mean that already, long before Jones' time, it had made its way from India to Western Europe through translations into Persian,

Arabic, Hebrew, Latin, and then the Western European languages. It was not alone in this. Another collection of Sanskrit fables from about the same time, the *Book of the Seven Wise Counsellors* as it came to be known, made its way via Arabic, Hebrew, and Latin, as far west as Ireland; and there is an Irish poem of the seventeenth or early eighteenth century, paraphrased in part by Swift (*The Festival of O'Rourke*, this incomplete version is called) which is said to refer to the 'Seven Wise Masters' as if they had become familiar figures of folk tradition in Ireland.[60]

The metaphysical sophistication of the Brahmin tradition obviously put a difficulty in the translator's path of quite another order from anything he encountered in Persian or Arabic; just as the complexities of the Hindu pantheon imposed a great difficulty as well. Since you must already have in mind that the literary world seems to have been a good deal more affected by the Orient very shortly after it was first opened up in a cultural sense, than it was later, and that this first phase of interest and enquiry has not, in the fullest sense, born fruit as might have been expected, you may by now be wondering whether it was these very difficulties which brought that about. But if there were difficulties, they were early overcome, at least to an impressive degree. In the very years when Jones was actually learning Sanskrit, Sir Charles Wilkins, the first Englishman really to master Sanskrit (he had gone out to India in 1770 as a writer to the East India Company), published an accurate and also perfectly readable and coherent translation of the *Baghavadgita*, the series of dialogues from the second century BC which might perhaps be described as the Pauline Epistles of Hinduism. Blake knew this work, and dedicates No. 10 of his *Descriptive Catalogue* to it:

> The subject is, Mr Wilkin translating the Geeta; an ideal design, suggested by the first publication of that part of the Hindu Scripture translated by Mr Wilkin.

Southey has many extracts from this work in his Common-Place Book, and its text appears a number of times in his voluminous notes to *Kehama*. Speaking more generally, there are also a number of passages in Blake's works where some knowledge on his part of Hindu thought may easily be recognized. Mr. Naravutty, for example, has pointed out that the Hindu myth that the universe was spun by a giant spider appears in the *First Book of Urizen* (viii. 6), and again twice in *The Four Zoas*. Blake seems to know quite intimately the creation myth from the *Bedang Shastra* as retold in Dow's *History of Hindustan*. 'Without contraries there is no progression' may not be very distinctive in itself, but it is close to Dow's account, and Blake's three states of Eden, Ulro and Beulah seem much like Dow's account of the successive development that follows, in the Hindu myth, from the initial contraries. Again, the four persons (shall one say) of the Hindu creator in this myth are closely paralleled by Blake's notion of fourfold being, embodied in Tharmas, Luvah, Urizen and Urthona. There are other more local or detailed parallels, but these suffice to make the point clear.[61]

Early in the nineteenth century there are other trans-
lations: though on the whole there are surprisingly few.
Thomas Broughton's versions from modern spoken
Hindi poems—*Selections from the Popular Poetry of the
Hindus* (1814), is of interest not only for the fresh lyrical
gaiety of some of the poems, but also because (like
Gladwin with respect to Persian) Broughton shows an
exact understanding of the metrical basis of the lyrics he
translates, and discusses it at length in his Preface. This
Preface also confirms how the employees of the East
India Company find Persian and Arabic more useful
than Hindi; which on the whole, says Broughton, is
neglected by the British. His own knowledge of Hindi
he acquired from the Sepoys—Sipahees—under his
command, and it is from them too that he learnt his
poems. His little collection is an exceptional one, however.

In the same year, Horace Hayman Wilson, a doctor
in the service of the Company (later Professor of Sanskrit at Oxford) published a translation (in very eighteenth-century heroic couplets) of a famous poem by
Kalidasa, the *Megha Duta* or *Cloud Messenger*. In this
poem a Hindu demigod or Yacsha, exiled by his super-
ior, entreats one of the clouds of the monsoon season,
pursuing its journey far inland, to act as a messenger to
his beloved wife. There is a very fair likelihood that
Shelley knew this poem, and used it when he wrote his
own poem on *The Cloud*, six years later. Not that he
can be said to follow the Sanskrit original. Shelley's
poem is given to the cloud itself to speak, and it is a
vision, deeply infused with the scientific thought of

Shelley's time, of a cloud's journeyings as part of the whole inter-working system of land and ocean and atmosphere. But it seems quite likely that he found his general idea in the Hindu poet's account of a cloud's journey over every kind of terrain and scenery; and there is one much more distinctive link which increases this likelihood. At one point in his poem, Shelley thinks of the stars that might show through a rent in the cloud, and mades the cloud say:

> . . . I laugh to see them whirl and flee
> Like a swarm of golden bees.
>
> (ll. 53–54)

Professor Piper has pointed out that this passage may owe something to a passage in Wordsworth's *Excursion*, Book IV: a famous passage from which the later Romantic poets seem generally to have quarried.[61a] Wordsworth, in the lines in question, describes primitive man's vision of the sun-god in the sky, and then the moon-goddess, sweeping along with her attendants:

> as moon and stars
> Glance rapidly along the clouded heavens
> When winds are blowing strong.
>
> (ll. 869–71)

There is Shelley's general idea of the stars as they, not the clouds, seem to move. The vivid, highly distinct image of the bees, however, is something quite new. But the Sanskrit poet has a parallel to it. He, at one point, thinks of how the evening worshippers, feeling the grateful showers from the cloud, might turn their eyes towards it—their eyes, he writes:

Whose glances gleam like bees along the sky

Wilson, in a note, draws attention to this striking image, and its newness to European poetry. Perhaps Shelley found in it what he adapted to his different but equally striking comparison between the stars and the golden bees.

As the century wore on, there came a change. In 1835, Dean Milman published some very readable versions from the *Mahabharata* and *Ramayana*. But he says that he in effect learnt Sanskrit in order to attempt to fill a gap: specialist scholars alone had contact with Sanskrit literature, and this meant that there was no contact of a kind really to stimulate poets. 'In this country, the students of oriental literature, endowed with taste and feeling for poetry, are so few in number': Sir William Jones, and Horace Wilson, were the only ones worth a mention. In 1852 Ralph Griffith published a collection of translations not only from the great epics (including the *Baghavad Gita*, which is a section of the *Mahabharata*) from *Sakontala*, and from the *Gita Govinda*, all of which had been translated before; but also from the great early masterpieces of Sanskrit, the *Laws of Manu* and the *Vedic Hymns*. But Griffith too, in his *Preface*, hints at neglect of Sanskrit verse on the part of the English public, and a shortage of available translations; in particular, he notes that Wilson's *Cloud Messenger* is readily available only to scholars, and that Dean Milman's book is out of print.

Griffith also gives us the necessary clue. It is hardly to be expected, he says, that many will be willing to master Sanskrit for the sake of its poetry—'in these utili-tarian times'.[62] The times were indeed 'utilitarian'; and this had a particular relevance to India and its culture.

It is quite impossible, in fact, to escape the conclu-sion that in the second quarter of the nineteenth century, there was in effect something like a slow recession of interest in the Hindu world. The work of scholars con-tinued, though not on the scale promised by the early decades of British rule in the sub-continent. But it did not become, to use Matthew Arnold's word, solidary with our culture. It did not impinge, in the way it once had, on the work of the poets or on the general quality of taste. Many factors contributed to this change, and on the whole they lie outside the present discussion. There were the difficulties of British administrators in India, encountering the many evils and abuses of con-temporary Indian life and being obliged to pre-occupy themselves with these (enthusiasm for Indian culture in Germany flourished better, because it had no consular side: it could take the ideal and ignore the real that embodied it). There was the pressure of missionaries to to be allowed to convert freely, which (as so often) went along with emphatic repudiation of the indige-nous religion as simply the work of Satan. There was also the development of a class of westernized Indians, who themselves wanted to adopt European culture and jettison their own; and the discovery of more primitive or debased forms of Hinduism, as more backward areas of the sub-continent were opened up to Europeans. All these factors, and doubtless others also, contributed to a swing of attitude, of which the decisive expression is

Macaulay's famous Minute on Indian education of
1834.

Macaulay's position in this celebrated document is as
clear as he alone could make a position; and as, in
fact, he always did. It makes one think at times, I fear,
of what Oscar Wilde called 'the great evolutionary
principle of the survival of the vulgarest'. Griffith's
word 'utilitarian' is brought forcibly to mind. Bacon
and Locke in philosophy, Sir Isaac Newton in science,
are Macaulay's touchstones; and his ebullient brilliance
is engaging, if at times also embarrassing. He demands
to know whether the British can really disregard the
need in India, and beyond that the demand from the
Indians themselves, for instruction in European science,
philosophy, political economy and medicine; and can
proffer instead, to students who insisted on payment
for learning them, oriental languages and the erudition
they embody: 'history abounding with kings thirty feet
high, and reigns thirty thousand years long—Geogra-
phy, made up of seas of treacle and seas of butter . . .
absurd metaphysics, absurd physics, absurd theology'.
'I have never found an Orientalist', he writes, 'who
could deny that a single shelf of a good European
library was worth the whole native literature of India
and Arabia.' The situation in India, he asserted, was
at bottom like that in England in the time of the Renaissance. Then, the simple fact was that Greek and
classical Latin contained the best works available,
either in literature or in erudition. Rightly, they took
the place of medieval writings and all their defects. His
other parallel was with Russia in the eighteenth century,

brought out of pre-medieval barbarism by intensive application to the literature of the West. 'In the time of our grandchildren,' he added, 'may she not be pressing close on France and Britain in the career of improvement?' The question was more pertinent than he knew.

I am enough of an Englishman, Utilitarian, and vulgarian, to think that strictly from the position of an educationalist (which was the position he took up and was required by his duties to take up) Macaulay was right. He was, of course, successful in determining the policy of the East India Company. Moreover, had the British decided on the other policy, they would soon have been forced to change by pressure from the Indians themselves. But this was the beginning of a substantial and deep-seated change in our own culture: a change which lay outside Macaulay's terms of reference and which I am sure he did not see. For when we began to stress English culture as the right intellectual sustenance for India, we began also to lose vital contact, for ourselves, with India's indigenous culture; and to make our own, something self-contained and self-sealed. This explains a good deal—ultimately it explains the odious Ronnie in *A Passage to India*—and in particular it explains what might be termed the evanescence of the Indian influence in our poetry, as between say Keats and Tennyson.

I want at this point to recall my discussion of the Arabic influence. Probably the most celebrated poems in the whole of Arabic literature are the seven great Mo'alaqat *Odes* which date from the times before the prophet and the conquests which resulted from his career.[63] These, known as the Mo'alaqat or 'Suspended Poems' because of a legend that their great merits had caused them to be hung up in the mosque at Mecca, celebrate the world of the Arabs when they were simply men of indomitable courage, living the hard life of the desert, and engaged in tribal warfare or in others of the more primitive human pre-occupations. Technically speaking, the form of a 'suspended' ode is rigidly fixed. Each of these poems (and there were many more, less celebrated than the seven, which conformed to the same pattern) opens with the poet's describing a lonely desert scene in which the only signs of life were the vestiges of a deserted Arab encampment. From this austere beginning, the poet passes on to the journey he has made, the points of his camel or the charms of his mistress or mistresses, and other matters as the case may be. Jones translated the 'Seven Odes', with a paragraph, which I think became fairly well known since it seems often to be quoted, describing in some detail their rigid poetic form.[64] The metre of the poems is one of long lines in couplets, with rhymes sustained over long passages (or whole poems) in a way quite impossible in English.

Locksley Hall (1842) is written in long couplets— each line has eight stresses, which is very unusual in English—and these may have been suggested to Tennyson by translations from the 'Suspended Odes'; or, perhaps, translations from the Sanskrit epics, like those of Dean Milman. The Arabian source is the more likely, because the opening scene of *Locksley Hall* is perhaps as near as an English poet, and an English

77

scene, could get to the conventional opening of the 'Suspended Ode':

> Comrades, leave me here a little, while as yet tis
> early morn
> Leave me here, and when you want me, sound upon the
> bugle horn
>
> Tis the place, and all around it, as of old, the curlews call,
> Dreary gleams about the moorland flying over Locksley
> Hall;

Tennyson may have been thinking of a particular house in Lincolnshire, and this may possibly explain why he goes on to set the terrain as he does; but the next line of Locksley Hall seems in a more general way to bring us again into touch with these famous desert poems:

> Locksley Hall, that in the distance overlooks *the sandy tracts*.

Moreover, there are one or two other, minor links between this poem and one in particular among the 'Suspended Odes'.[65]

But in this poem Tennyson also has in mind other aspects of the Orient. The speaker is the orphan child of a man who met his death in 'wild Mahratta-battle' (this refers of course to the campaigns in the northern Deccan) and thinks of finding a refuge in the East for his troubled and confused life. But in this respect, the East affords the poet only a superficial, a largely scenic image. Today, one would relate it to picture-postcards rather than any real contact with an exotic culture. It is a matter of 'larger constellations burning, mellow moons and happy skies', of 'lustrous woodlands', luxuriant climbing plants, the 'heavy-fruited tree', the 'heavy-blossomed bower', parrots calling, rainbow-coloured streams. In fact, all the things which offer simply an escape from the only civilization which the poem recognizes: steamship, railway, and 'the march of mind'. And the link between this externalized and unsympathetic attitude to the East, and the work and attitude of the missionaries which I mentioned before, is perhaps stressed in the line in which the poem begins the movement of thought which repudiates the line of escape, once it has been considered:

> But I count the *gray barbarian* lower than the *Christian child*.

Perhaps it is to the point that in *Locksley Hall Sixty Years After*, written in the mid 1880's, there is once again a purely literary echo of the Suspended-Ode convention in the opening—'Late, my grandson! Half the morning have I paced these sandy tracts' and so on —but that the only references otherwise to the East are to 'crushing the Moslem in his pride' and to the line (if so it must be called):

Russia bursts our Indian barrier, shall we fight her? shall we yield?

In Tennyson's last collection, *The Death of Oenone*, 1892, there is another poem set in the Orient: *Akbar's Dream*.[66] Here also, at the very end of his life, Tennyson shows that, in a sense, the subject retains his interest. The Hymn which closes the poem is in a typically Persian or Arabic metre and stanza form, and Akbar himself is of course the great Mogul Emperor who was an almost exact contemporary of Queen Elizabeth I.

But the historical fact of Akbar's willingness to treat the various religions of his great empire with tolerance is translated by Tennyson into wholly nineteenth-century terms:

> I can but lift the torch
> Of Reason in the dusty cave of life
> And gaze on this great miracle the world:
> Adoring that who made, and makes, and is,
> And is not, what I gaze on—all else, form,
> Ritual, varying with the tribes of men

Akbar's ultimate interest sounds remarkably like Arnold's 'the not ourselves which makes for righteousness'. Elsewhere in the poem, what one senses is something like a nineteenth-century 'Higher Pantheism'—that phrase, of course, is the title of another of Tennyson's poems.

But even insofar as Tennyson does represent the East in his poem, he repudiates it at the end. Akbar's son sweeps away his régime of enlightened toleration, and the poem reverts to the East as the perennial home of tyranny:

> The shriek and curse of trampled millions
> As in time before . . .

I mentioned this in my last lecture as one of the clichés of thought about the Orient.

Finally, the poem ends with what Tennyson sees as the true salvation of India:

> From out the sunset poured an alien race,
> Who fitted stone to stone again, and Truth,
> Peace, Love and Justice came and dwelt therein.

Tennyson adds that the aliens from the west abolished suttee, child-marriage and perpetual widowhood into the bargain. It only remained for him to add a reference to clubs, tennis, milky tea, and not being able to speak foreign languages, to complete the picture as we have it in E. M. Forster's novel. In effect the poem ends with Akbar's blessing of the westerners who accomplish what his own peoples could not accomplish for themselves.

In these acts of repudiation—cursory, half-intended if you like as they seem—one can sense something that goes in the end far beyond the frontiers merely of literature. There is no doubt that when we first went into India we proposed to ourselves to master its cultures; and our achievement in this direction was soon a very remarkable one. But later in the nineteenth century there was something like a progressive alienation from the culture which before very long was to escape from our control. It seems as if, in our own particular case, having once been cosmopolites of *power* if one may so put it, in the process of ceasing to be *that*, we had also, in part at least, to cease to be cosmopolites of culture. It was Jones who said, in the 1780's, 'wherever we direct our attention to Hindu literature, the notion of infinity presents itself'. But 100 or 150 years later, this same sense of the metaphysical profundity, even obscurity, of the Hindu tradition may be found more easily in the work of those who belonged to other national cultures; in the writings of Paul Elmer More, for example,[67] or in the 'Asiatic vague immensities' of which Yeats speaks in his poem *The Statues*. Neither of these particular references are sympathetic, as Jones's was. But in Yeats, taking his work generally, we can find a considered and pondered sense of traditional Indian culture, and its importance, such as could not well be matched in the work of any major English poet of Yeats's own time.

Paul Elmer More, along with Irving Babbitt, was once in a class of two at Harvard with C. R. Lanman, the Professor of Sanskrit. Some years later T. S. Eliot also attended Lanman's class; and Professor Daiches has pointed out to me that Eliot's Sanskrit passage in Part V of *The Waste Land* is contained in a fable from one of the *Upanishads* which Lanman re-tells in an essay dated 1913.[68] In this fable the supreme God is asked by Gods, men, and demons, to give them instruction; and to each, it seems, he utters one and the same word: Da—which is 'What the thunder said' in Eliot's poem. But the three classes of beings receive the message differently: they hear, each in their turn, the words control, give, and show pity: dámyata, dattá dayádhvam. Each of them, from the one self-same word, learns the lesson which is appropriate for his own order of created being. The fable ends with a turn of thought that explains the title of this part of the poem: when the thunder rolls, the noise it makes is simply da, da, da. But the message is there all the same. Just listen, and you can take the message appropriate to you. This explains the word DA repeated thrice in the passage in Eliot's poem. As for the word 'shantih', which comes three times to close the whole work, this refrain (as I know from having heard it sung) is the refrain which closes the Sanskrit service for the burial of the dead: in other words, Eliot is saying 'in my end is my beginning' as he was to do again later in his work. The first section of the poem is entitled 'The burial of the Dead' and in the 'peace' of the closing line (shantih means peace) the process is brought successfully to an end.

Moreover, the water-symbol (both the rain that falls when the thunder speaks at last, and the spring water imagined in various ways throughout this closing section of the Waste Land) is closely bound up in the poem with the divine teaching uttered by the thunder. Dattá, give, is the message for the human plane of existence, and Lanman explains in his essay that the pouring of water was traditionally seen as the proper symbolical accompaniment of making a gift—for the reason, it seems, that once water is poured out it cannot be drawn back again, and so is truly of the nature of a gift. At all events, when all these points are taken into account, the closing section of the poem presents a much more integrated and sequacious appearance than it does otherwise. But this does not argue against, and in a way it actually supports, the point I made earlier on: for Eliot, when he wrote this poem, was not an English poet, and was not drawing on anything that English culture had given him.

IV. THE FAR EAST: EGYPT: SOME CONCLUSIONS

*T*here was a good deal of interest in China in the eighteenth century and indeed in the later part of the seventeenth century; but it was of a distinctive kind. The wonders described or embellished by Marco Polo —the Great Khan's hill of lapis lazuli forested with trees that were transplanted fullgrown, his retinues of feasting nobles with their 150,000 banqueting robes, all a gift from himself, his 5,000 falcons and 10,000 hunting hounds and all the rest of it—these things are not what preoccupied later Orientalists. Addison is interested in the Chinese, in his papers on landscape, for the elegant naturalness of their planted parks, their modest and restrained art that is made to seem like nature. In *Spectator* papers 584–5 he recounts what he alleges to be a Chinese fable, and the interest he displays is much of the same kind. 'I shall here translate', he says '[a letter from the hero to the heroine] without departing from the noble simplicity of Sentiments, and Plainness of manners, which appears in the original.' Sir William Temple, in the second section of his essay *Of*

Heroic Virtue, gives an account mainly of the political structure and customs of the Chinese. His description of the thought of Confucius, which is really quite well-informed, carries the same emphasis. He fully realizes how Confucius' fundamental concern as a philosopher was with political and social structure and values, and he also sees the importance of the concept of natural reason in Confucius' thought, and of the law of nature as the ultimate principle upon which social and political life is organized if it is healthy. The same stress reappears in Goldsmith's *Citizen of the World* (1762). The antecedents of this work are complex. In it, a serenely wise Oriental surveys and criticizes English life in a series of letters written to a friend at home. This may be traced directly back to the *Persian Letters* of Lord Lyttelton of 1735, which themselves imitated the *Lettres Persanes* of Montesquieu, which appeared in 1721 and created something of a European sensation. These in their turn may be referred back[69] to the first literary document of this kind, the *Espion Turc* collection, published by Giovanni Marana in French in 1684, later translated into English (probably, it seems, by Marana himself in part, under a pseudonym). This translation was widely influential on the English periodical essay of the early eighteenth century. Defoe had already used the idea of a Chinese as critic of European society. Goldsmith takes the name of the recipient of his own Chinese Letters from one of the Oriental pseudo-collections of the period, the *Chinese Tales*, and he knew Horace Walpole's Letter, dated 1757, from a Chinese sage frivolously entitled *Xo Ho*.

It is in Letter 33 of the *Citizen of the World* that Gold-smith's general position is made clear. His Chinese sage finds the English quite unwilling to learn the truth about Chinese life. They know already. 'The true Eastern style', for them, is one 'where nothing more is required but sublimity'. 'Eastern tales should always be sonorous, lofty, musical and unmeaning.' They are disappointed that Goldsmith's Chinese speaks only like themselves, 'mere chit chat and common sense'. In this letter Goldsmith, when he is speaking seriously, rejects one conventional account of the Oriental style. He stresses the East as the home not of the extravagant but the ethical. 'In the East, similes are seldom used, and metaphor almost wholly unknown; but in China particularly . . . a cool phlegmatic mode of writing pre-vails . . . the writers, ever more assiduous to instruct than to please, address rather the judgment than the fancy.'

This conception of Chinese culture was in no way swept aside when, in the early nineteenth century, ac-counts of that country began to be written in English by men who had a first-hand knowledge of its way of life and its language. One of the earliest general accounts was J. F. Davis's *The Chinese*, published in the *Library of Entertaining Knowledge* in 1836. This series appeared in parallel with the *Library of Useful Know-ledge*, in which Davis's work would surely have ap-peared, if 1836 had been the same as 1966. A promi-nent part of the book is a translation of nearly a hundred Chinese proverbs, throughout which the emphasis is on moral wisdom for the conduct of personal and social

86

life;[70] and Davis also give great emphasis to the concept of filial piety as the basis of all Chinese conduct.

But these early Chinese scholars were frequently missionaries; and their interest in Chinese civilization had, perhaps inevitably, something of the external, of the critical. The parallel with British attitudes in India after the beginning of the nineteenth century is obvious enough; and something of the same kind persisted later in the century, when professional English scholars of Chinese began to open up Chinese literature and drama to the West. Davis knew something of the Chinese theatre, and gives an interesting account, seemingly firsthand, of theatrical productions in Macao. He knows about the indifference to realistic illusion, the splendid costumes but absence of scenery, and the stylized conventions for indicating locality. But his mind is utterly closed to the idea that these conventions might have real dramatic power. For him they are 'odd expedients . . . not many degrees above Nick Bottom (in the *Midsummer Night's Dream*)'. He is able, however, to give a clear account of the *Shŷ King*,[71] the collection of early Chinese verse which Pound, of course, was later to translate as 'The Classic Anthology Defined by Confucius'. Davis knows that this collection has four parts, and in a mechanical sense his descriptions of these are correct and informed. But 'the bulk of these curious vestiges of antiquity in China do not rise beyond the most primitive simplicity'.

At the end of the nineteenth century, when Japanese culture was beginning to become known, partly through its Nō drama of the fifteenth century, much the same attitude shows again. As early as 1883, that extraordinarily picturesque figure of journalism, exoticism, and travel, Lafcadio Hearn, is writing his essay called 'A Peep at Japanese Poetry', and speaking almost in the same breath of its 'purity and simple beauty' and of its 'charming naif' quality, its 'artless expressions' or its 'very pretty sentiment'; and the relevance at this point of Gilbert and Sullivan's *Mikado* (1885) is obvious enough. Edwin Arnold, writing in the 1880's on the basis of having lived in Japan for some years, is to some extent an exception. He calls the Nō 'entirely classical, traditional and complicated by allusion', and adds 'A Parisian or Viennese *pas-seul* became clumsy athleticism matched with it.'[72] But this last phrase also makes clear the limitations of his standpoint: he does not speak of Nō as drama at all, but merely of the Nō *dance*. In general, in this early period, those who are able to see the Nō as a form of drama, do so only with much condescension. Professor B. H. Chamberlin, writing on the *Classical Poetry of the Japanese* in 1880, knows about the Nō plays as 'lyric dramas', knows that they employ no scenery, a statuesque mode of acting, and a recitative style in delivery, but this is simply 'by no means unpleasing' once one gets used to it, and the dancing is 'tedious and meaningless to the European spectator'. Professor W. G. Aston, in his *History of Japanese Literature* (1899), condescends from a considerable height: the plays are 'not without charm in spite of being deficient in lucidity, method, coherence and good taste'. 'The reader who has the patience will not go altogether unrewarded.'

Such an attitude was to continue for some years. A. Lloyd, writing in 1908 and 1910, says that the Japanese who have taught him stress the 'suggestiveness of the Nō plays, and their 'moral discipline'; but for himself, 'their extraordinary popularity during the last few years is hardly merited'.[73]

These last words, however, of course reveal the fact that some major change had occurred. In part, this interest seems to have been aroused by Japanese in London who spoke of and lectured on the Nō drama, and by the visit of a Japanese *Kabuki* company to London in 1901 (*Kabuki* is a later form of Japanese drama than Nō, and spectacular, even melodramatic, by comparison with it). Max Beerbohm reviewed their performances with enthusiasm and even reverence; and by now a change of attitude begins to be clear. Osman Edwards, in 1901, is a curious mixture of the old tone and the new. 'Let us not apply to these (plays) the standard of *mature* drama, demanding situation, character, plot, movement. Rather compare them with the miracle plays and mysteries of the Chester or Coventry collections.' But on the other hand, he writes: 'the palm of sacred drama for beauty, interest and pathos must be awarded to the Nō'.[74] Such a contrast between the mature and the sacred presumably raises more issues than it settles; but the note of genuine insight and sympathy is unmistakable.

It is one of the paradoxes of literary history—they are not infrequent, and occasionally reward the scholar when little else does—that the first person of British race who had a more or less satisfactory notion of what the

Nō plays were like, and also set on them the high value that was later to be set on them by Yeats and Pound, was no professional academic or professional writer, but Marie Stopes. Marie Stopes, besides her other and better known interests, was a minor poet, and a resident in Japan for about a year and a half. Her account of and evaluation of the Nō plays first appeared in a paper she read to the Royal Society of Literature in November 1909 (it is reprinted in the Society's *Proceedings*). Her book, *Plays of Old Japan*, did not appear until 1913. Marie Stopes clearly crossed the frontier between super-cilious interest or grudging praise on the one hand, and whole-hearted commitment on the other. In spite of a somehow amateurist tone in her writing—a misogynist will detect traces of the womanishly gushing, and Pro-fessor Lloyd is a little sarcastic at her expense—she clearly recognizes the extraordinary beauty and subtle variety of these works: the allusive delicacy of the text, and the 'dignity and impersonalness of the actors', as she puts it. She is utterly free from realistic criteria of drama derived from William Archer or the plays of Pinero. (Professor Lloyd's observations, which I quoted just now, were an old-fashioned kind of retort to her.) But she accepts Nō on its own terms.

> The details of the literary style and composition are beyond the reach of my judgment . . . but of the atmosphere and general effect I can judge for myself, and I find them among the supremely great things of world literature.[75]

Ernest Fenollosa's account of the Nō drama is, in its technical details, immensely more sophisticated than that of Marie Stopes. No doubt also, his views were formed quite independently of hers; perhaps, in private, they were formed earlier. In the essay by Fenollosa which Pound printed in *Nō or Accomplishment* (1916), based on Fenollosa's notes, the endorsement of Nō is inward and wholehearted:

> A form of drama as primitive, as intense, and almost as beautiful as the ancient Greek drama at Athens, still exists in the world. (p. 101)

But all the same, it is right that Marie Stopes' modest but genuine place in this process of discovery should be recorded.

To my mind, indeed, it is a passage in her account of this drama which affords the clearest clue as to why and how Nō received the enthusiastic endorsement which at this time it did receive. She emphasizes the peculiar nature of this drama. It makes, she suggests, an appeal to the audience which is multiple and complex, yet intimately delicately unified at the same time. It offers, that is to say, an experience of a subtle and unusual kind. Here is an abridgement of her account of it:

> Also working on the . . . audience . . . is the psychic effect of the beautiful and harmonious colouring and of the potent music . . . to this effect the audience of the Nō is preeminently exposed, for all the surrounding conditions are calculated to enhance and aid it . . . the beautiful simplicity and harmony of the colour scheme . . . dignity and impersonalness of the actors . . . allusions and suggestions of the poems . . . descriptions of natural beauties

> . . . religious and philosophical ideas . . . when *combined*
> *with* the strange and solemn music . . . create *together*
> within the heart of the observer *a something which is well*
> *nigh sublime.*

Some of you may already have caught the echo which
came into my mind when first I read those words[76]:

> . . . when *all are together,* moon and wave and whiteness and
> setting Time and the last melancholy cry, they evoke *an*
> *emotion which cannot be evoked by any other* arrangement of
> colours and sounds and forms.

This is Yeats, in an essay called 'The Symbolism of
Poetry' (1900), describing the peculiarly intricate unity
of the experience offered to us by some uniquely poignant lines from Burns. That the lines are from Burns
is not to the point; what is to the point is how Yeats
concludes his argument:

> We may call this metaphorical writing, but it is better to
> call it *symbolical* writing.

Yeats was describing what he took at this time, and
what the French Symbolist poets like Rimbaud and
Mallarmé had taken before him, as the very essence of
the poetic experience. And if the similarity between
the Yeats passage, and that from Marie Stopes, is clear,
then the special reason why Nō drama could speak so
immediately and eloquently to the literary intelligentsia
of the period must be clear also. The Nō, in its subtle
and intimate fusion of poetry, song, music, dance and
mime-spectacle, also offered a *symboliste* kind of experience. It was, in fact, much more ambitious, complex

and historically venerable a *Symboliste* drama than ever that of Maeterlinck, for example, could be. In 1910, Nō could draw the Symboliste-influenced English poets much as the complexities of the Wagnerian aesthetic experience—spectacle, music, libretto interwoven with an intimacy new, or thought new, in opera—drew the French poets of a generation earlier.

The historical associations of modern or modernist poetry are not my immediate concern; but one of the more notable paradoxes of this movement cannot but emerge now into view; and if we try to understand why this particular paradox came into being, we indeed find that another line of thought, traceable to the influence of another exotic culture, in part explains it. It was the French *Symbolistes* who looked back to Edgar Allan Poe as the founder of their movement; and Carlyle, with his associations to the English and the German Romantics, who first enunciated in English a philosophical doctrine of reality as everywhere Symbolic, as everywhere an interwoven mesh of symbols pointing beyond the reality of the senses. Carlyle gave expression, in discursive form, to the outlook of the French *Symbolistes*, and that of Yeats too. It is also the case that a neo-platonist, even occultist tradition runs back from Yeats, through the French poets, and re-appears in major figures of the English Romantic period like Shelley, and more particularly Blake. The other line of 'Romantic' development, through Tennyson, to the writers like William Watson, Alfred Noyes, and the other versifiers of the turn of the century against whom the new poets in England were most emphatically reacting, was in the fact a much less authentic and more diluted line of development from the first and great phase of Romanticism.

How then could symbolist poetry—or as it should properly be called, post-symbolist poetry in England—take an anti-romantic form? Part of the explanation lies in the indirect influence, at this precise point of time, of another 'exotic' culture: that of ancient Egypt. Ancient Egypt began to be really important with the foundation of the Egyptian Exploration Fund in the 1880's and the work of Edouard Naville and Flinders Petrie. It began to make its own new and distinctive demands on aesthetic thinking, and also to align itself, or so it seemed, with the new influence of early Byzantine art, the art of the icon above all, coming in more or less at the same time. One can find an English poet responding, in a general way, to the quality of Egyptian megalithic sculpture as early as Shelley's sonnet *Ozymandias* of 1817; but this was really to the archeological *landscape* of classical Egypt, not to any sustained contemplation of the sculpture face to face. Shelley was not interested in the distinctively *aesthetic* experience which it offered. But in Wilhelm Worringer's *Abstraction and Empathy* of 1908 (written in 1906) we find a crystallization of aesthetic theories which had been developing in Germany from the 1880's, partly under the influence of Egyptian and Byzantine megalithic sculpture considered in themselves.

Worringer distinguished two fundamental ways in which the artist could approach the reality out of which he made his art. On the one hand, he could identify

94

himself with the natural world, could find in it something which answered his own feelings and aspirations,
something which seemed to him to mirror his subjec-
tive emotions, and be readily and happily acceptable
for its beauty and vitality. From this response would
spring an art of what Worringer called 'reverent affir-
mation of the phenomenal world'; an art with, as its
principal method, the naturalistic reproduction of that
world's varied beauty. This was what Worringer found
above all in Greek art and what he called classical. But
there was another kind; based on a fundamentally different kind of approach to the natural world, which he
called 'the transcendental feeling towards the world'.
This feeling and its products in art Worringer viewed
in the following terms:

> a . . . psychic function which, *remote* from all reverent
> affirmation of the phenomenal world, seeks to create for
> itself a picture of things that shifts them far beyond the
> finiteness and conditioning of the living into a zone of the
> necessary and abstract. Inextricably drawn into the vicissi-
> tudes of ephemeral appearances, the soul knows here only
> *one* possibility of happiness, that of creating a world beyond
> appearance, an absolute, in which it may rest from the
> agony of the relative.[77]

Such a transcendental attitude to reality Worringer saw
as producing a stylized, formalized art, of which the
sculpture of ancient Egypt was the grand and definitive
example; though in his later work (*Formprobleme der
Gothick*, 1912), he sees medieval sculpture—'the product of non-reconciliation to the outer world'—as
another example. Here was 'abstraction' from the world

95

of the senses, as the life-loving, naturalistic art of the Greeks was 'empathy' towards it.

The anti-Romanticism of the new poets of about 1910—I have of course Pound and Eliot in mind, for Yeats was never an anti-Romantic—is partly the result of their interest in the verse of the early seventeenth century. Such an interest, such an admiration, as Professor Duncan and Professor Kathleen Tillotson have shown, has a substantial nineteenth-century history, and goes clearly back to (among much else) Charles Lamb's *Preface* to his *Specimens of the English Dramatic Poets* of 1808. But anti-Romanticism is also to be linked with T. E. Hulme's acquaintance (of a somewhat sketchy kind, it seems) with the theories of Worringer and his earlier contemporary Theodor Lipps. Hulme, himself a Roman Catholic, naturally admired the art of the middle ages, and accepted the account of Worringer which gave it theoretical validity. But Hulme was no art historian. He was much more at home with the catch-phrases of critical polemic than with the detail of works of art known first hand. The art which Worringer considered to issue from the transcendental attitude to reality was a rational, contemplative art, formal and unemotional. In quite other contexts, the term 'classical' had been appropriated for art of this kind. Hulme happily appropriated it over again. If transcendental art then was classical, what was naturalistic art, which Worringer, indeed, had called classical, but which he had set in opposition to transcendental? Obviously, it was Romantic. This identification, or rather this somersaulting of the identifications of Worringer, emerges quite clearly in Hulme's essay 'On Classical and Romantic', in *Speculations*, where there is also a general salute in the direction of Worringer. Its paradoxical implication, of course, was that the sculpture of the classical world was romantic; and had Hulme wanted to push his thinking in that direction, he would doubtless have had to think again. But his interests lay elsewhere; and the aesthetic theories of Worringer became a stick to beat Keats and Shelley. Here, then, is one cause of the paradoxical fact that by the time it had come down to T. S. Eliot, the Symbolist Movement, with its origins in Romanticism, had become anti-Romantic.

I was speaking just now of the growth of interest in Japanese Nō drama during the 1900's and early 1910's. Of course, the writer whom this above all concerned was Yeats. But it is really rather doubtful whether the Nō was a fundamental influence on Yeats. It is clear enough that a play like *At the Hawks Well*, which Yeats wrote immediately after his first contact with the Japanese drama, contains unmistakable traces of Nō technique. But at the same time, these are fully in continuity with methods of writing and of presentation which had been his own long before. Even as early as the *Letters to the New Island*, published in newspapers in the United States before 1890, Yeats had come down once for all on the side of a non-naturalistic drama aiming at subtle suggestiveness, and presented in a formalized, even incantatory verse and acting style. Nothing is further from the truth than any idea that Yeats could snatch at something he found in an exotic culture, and exploit it as if exploiting meant some kind of surface cleverness, some writer's trick-of-the-trade. The Nō could speak from far outside, because it spoke to what was already deep within.

There is a beautiful illustration of this, which has never, I believe, been fully worked out. *Purgatory*, written more than twenty years after Yeats encountered the Nō, contains a passage, or perhaps I should say an incident, which surely looks back to his study of Nō. At the end of the play, as the Old Man and his son struggle for the money, the window of the ruined house is suddenly lit up, and the ghostly image of the Old Man's own father is seen at the lighted window. But this is simply one ghost dreaming of another. It is:

> . . . the impression upon my *mother's* mind . . .

says the Old Man. And later:

> And *she* must animate that dead night
> Not once but many times

The couple enjoy this phantasmal meeting as part of what Yeats, in his own terminology, would have called the mother's *Dreaming Back*. But now turn to Pound's translation (following Fenollosa) of the *Nishikigi*:

> Strange, what seemed so very old a cave
> Is all glittering-bright within,
> Like the flicker of fire.
> It is like the inside of a house . . .
> Is it illusion, illusion?

Illusion, in a sense, of course it is: the *impression*, in Yeats's phrase, *upon a mind*. But here too in *Nishikigi*, the

98

man and the woman, no ghosts, must undergo a series of meetings:

> To dream under dream we return.
> Three years . . . And the meeting comes now!
> This night has happened over and over,
> And only now comes the tryst.

Theatrical effect, human situation, and metaphysical interpretation, are all much the same in the two plays.[78]

But the main point of interest in this scene in the Yeats play has not yet transpired. It begins to transpire only when we turn to quite another area of Yeats's indebtedness—one also little explored, I believe, at least by English, by non-Irish scholars—and notice that the movement of thought in the opening stanzas of *Among School Children* conforms fairly closely to one of the best-known poetic forms of the last phase of native Irish poetry, the *aisling* of the eighteenth century, the penal age in Ireland. The *aisling* was a kind of ode in which the poet, after experiencing some everyday scene, finds himself in the presence of a woman of surpassing beauty, at first anonymous. Well, compare *Among School Children*. *Sailing to Byzantium* is also, and in two respects, reminiscent of the native Irish poetry of this century. First, its opening stanza, the rejection of the country of boundless sensuous beauty and fertility, sounds like first a rehearsal, and then a rejection, of the traditional celebration of the beauty and fertility of the land of Ireland itself. This tradition may be found, for example, in Egan O'Rahilly's *Epithalamium for Lord Kenmare*:[79] This marriage took place in 1720. Another example is the poem of Owen Roe O'Sullivan quoted in translation by Daniel Corkery in his work *The Hidden Ireland*:

> ... the choiring birds on the green tree branches, the sea birds and fish swimming from the tide, the swan brightly taking the wave's crest ...[80]

with which compare Yeats:

> ... birds in the trees
> (Those dying generations) at their song,
> The salmon falls, the mackerel crowded seas.

The likeness is clear, and if the matter be pursued using Yeats's drafts for his poem,[81] the parallels become so numerous as to be absolutely beyond question. Owen Roe O'Sullivan was the author of the most famous of all the eighteenth century Irish *aislings*, and I believe one of the most famous of all lyric poems in the Irish language—the poem often called by its opening words, 'Brightness of brightness', in English. I think Yeats had this too in his mind or at the back of it, when writing *Sailing to Byzantium*:

> Through many an hour and day did I follow and follow
> Till I reached the *magic palace* reared of old by Druid art

writes the earlier Irish poet. Owen Roe O'Sullivan's *aisling* also ends with a 'crossing the sea'. Yeats writes:

> And therefore have I sailed the seas and come
> To the holy city of Byzantium.

Yeats's celebration of the great house of the Anglo Irish ascendency (for example in *Meditations in Time of Civil War*), is strongly reminiscent of O'Rahilly's eulogy of a great house of the native Irish aristocracy in the *Elegy on O'Callaghan*.[82]

All this is by way of preliminary before I return to Yeats's *Purgatory*. I am sure that it is not to *Nishikigi* alone that his sources should be traced in this case. That extraordinary moment in *Purgatory* could come into existence because the exotic and the deeply native chanced to come, for a moment, into an extraordinary unity. That Yeats was in some sense well acquainted with the native Irish writing of the period (though his knowledge of the native language itself may have left much to be wished) cannot be disputed. His close friendship with Douglas Hyde, his enthusiastic co-operation with Hyde (in the years shortly after 1900) for the publishing of a veritable library of texts in this field, put all that beyond doubt. In particular, he certainly knew Hyde's *Songs Ascribed to Raftery* of 1903. Raftery was the blind hedge-poet and fiddler of the late eighteenth century who turns up, for example, in section ii of Yeats's *The Tower*, and Hyde's great technical skill as a verse translator produced English versions from which, in their most remarkable interplay of Greek mythology and vernacular diction, I myself think Yeats may have learnt a good deal; though I cannot say whether this very striking stylistic quality is in the Irish text, which I cannot yet read, nor if Yeats could have got it effectively from there, if it is. But it seems to me certain that Yeats studied at least the English versions, and that Raftery's poems were of some importance in the development of his rhetorical yet vigorously vernacular middle style. Then, one comes to Hyde's account of the close of Raftery's life:

> . . . many is the story I have heard about his death. An old man who had no English told me that he died alone by himself in an empty house without anyone being with him, but the house was all lighted up as bright as day . . . [83]

Perhaps it is time to generalize. Much and perhaps most of the work I have examined in these lectures has been below—sometimes much below—the first class. First-class work is rare. But where, in my own judgement, this has not been so, or least been so, it has repeatedly been the case that what was exotic has found some path into a deep alignment with what belonged to a meaningful indigenous tradition; or with some nodal point in the poet's own personal experience. And Yeats is not alone as an example. If the passage in *Nishikigi* struck a chord with the image of the great ruined houses of the Ascendency, and at the same time with the death of the blind hedge-poet of the penal age, there are other examples too. One is Shelley's *Mask of Anarchy*. Shelley celebrated the Massacre of Peterloo not only by hinting at a juggernaut procession such as he had read of in Southey's *Curse of Kehama* or a figure of the goddess of love that he drew from Jones's Hindu *Hymn to Camdeo*. These were the images of his poem, but he set them in the metre of an English street-ballad (this point is brought out in Pinto and Rodway's *The Common Muse*)[84] and in rhythms that remind the reader of the English volunteer militia themselves as they march along. The content may be exotic, the form belongs to the everyday life of our people as Shelley knew it. Wordsworth's Arabian in the Vision of *Prelude* Book V—that 'gentle dweller in the desert'—is a haunting and memorable figure, and reverberates in the imagination, because he is no Oriental Hajji Baba, but one, in personality, with the figures of *The Ruined Cottage* or *Guilt and Sorrow*. Wordsworth has endowed him with the calm and dignity, stolid yet infinitely unprosaic, which he was able to find in Michael and the leech gatherer and other people in his own rural experience. Finally, Arnold's *Sohrab and Rustum* is an oriental tale in its subject, but by no means in its treatment. For this, Arnold was drawing from deep within himself, and was also drawing from traditions which he found not only in the literary scene of the time, but also in its educational scene. That 'foiled circuitous wanderer' the mournful river Oxus, is an image of his own inner life and tensions; but the noble simplicity of the poem's action and diction, Arnold had drawn from the tradition of classical learning at its best (a tradition in which his own father has of course an outstanding place), and at the same time from the style of Wordsworth, which Arnold so deeply admired. I do not mean that the poem is beyond cavil in this respect. It does not seem to me a great poem. But clearly it is the work of a serious and distinguished poet, and is of enduring interest and importance; and I am arguing that, here as elsewhere, such work comes about when the exotic influence meets with, and weds with, substantial forces and continuities from within the poet himself and from within the indigenous traditions of his society.

I have used the word 'exotic' more than once in these lectures, and if it is taken in its strict sense it is wholly to the point. But in its strict sense it means simply, something that comes from a place outside. In that sense in which it means colourful and luxurious, it is a part, but only one part, of the story I have been trying to tell. In 1817, Jeffrey reviewed *Lalla Rookh* in the '*Edinburgh*'; and noted, in his characteristically dry but generous way, both the attraction, and the limit of attraction, of the exotic in the narrowly colourful sense. The poem is set in the Orient, and 'wantons luxuriously', he says, 'in those voluptuous regions'. He recognizes, freely, its profusion of 'barbaric ornaments'. But at the same time, he remains clearly conscious that there is something else which can get into a poem and which is altogether more important than any of these things; that the final effect of colour and extravagance and nothing else is to make a reader conscious only of emptiness and penury at another level:

> We rather think . . . the effect of the whole is to dazzle more than to enchant . . . by the constant succession of glittering images and high-strained emotions.[85]

John Foster, in and around 1817, was also regularly reviewing works with an oriental interest, and also condemning the extravagance, as he saw it, of the East. But this was at quite another level. Foster represents the missionary disapproval I spoke about earlier. Jeffrey was diagnosing a one-sidedness of appeal, or a surface without a deeper appeal. The same distinction could perfectly well have been made about a work with no exotic element whatever. Ultimately, we are facing, once again, the contrast which others have found between Spenser and Donne, or between Daniel and Drayton, and so on over the whole run of our poetry or indeed our literature.

English writers and poets have been drawn towards the widening horizons I have been discussing, not for colour and extravagance alone, but in almost every case for that other and solider thing as well. It was the mysterious wisdom of the Druids, as well as the wildness and magnificence of bardic verse, that captured their imaginations. It was not only the thrills and terrors of Norse mythology that they cared for, but also the iron rigour of its code, and the unsurpassable bluntness and terseness of its language. To illustrate my point further, I am tempted to contrast the Saxon idea, with its stress on liberty in institutions and valour in the defence of it, with romantic Arthurian mythology; but this would conceal how intricately the contrast I am drawing runs through the subject as a whole: the Arthurian world itself was one, according to legend, in which dour courage and stoicism were to be found as well as romance and enchantment. The closing books of Malory, with their account of the last battles and death of Arthur, set this beyond doubt. Similarly with the vogue of the Middle East in the eighteenth century. There was a distinction between the Arabian world as one of notable ethical quality and a notable way of life, rather in contrast to the luxurious beauty, glamorous colour, and amorous delicacy which were associated with Persia. But at the same time, Persia itself was seen in a double light. Besides its colour and so forth, it was also a place of serene ethical and political wisdom, and of the expression of these things in the fable, the apo-thegm, the quatrain, refined to simplicity not extrava-gance. It was this second way of thinking which meant that, after the main literary impact of the Orient on English poetry was in fact spent, and the period of alien-ation which I spoke of last time had set in, Fitzgerald in the *Rubaiyat* of Omar Kayyam—as he called it, though it is his own Rubaiyat as much as anyone else's—was able to turn the aphoristic and ethical side of the idea of Persia so much to his own ends. Indeed, the success of this work is one further illustration of the point I was making earlier. It is one further case of literary success where the exotic influence coincides with something deeply felt at home: in this case, the crisis in religious thought in the mid-nineteenth-century.

With India the same distinction is to be made. The *Curse of Kehama* must be set against the references by Sir William Jones and Dean Milman to the great *sim-plicity* of style of the Brahmins; and in Jones's own poetry influenced by Hindu thought and Sanskrit models, the rich luxuriance of effect is the one side, and the weighty core of philosophical thinking and reli-gious consciousness is the other. M. A. Hincks, in his work on the Japanese dance of 1910, is not uninterested in the magnificent costumes of the Nō actors, nor in the beauty of the spectacle; but what he emphasizes is that the dramas are subtly indirect expressions of Bud-dhist ethical teaching.[86]

I do not want to stress the necessity of a choice between these two kinds of interest. One of them, and one only, may suffice for life at the level of conduct. It will not readily suffice for art. No doubt the stress on these two dimensions of the literary art may vary a good deal as between the one extreme and the other. By the two extremes I mean the concept of literature, of poetry, as a regulator of life, for the one, and as an irruptor into life, a stimulator, exciter, opener-up of it, for the other. Neither, no doubt, will do by itself; but each—as any student of literature surely knows—tends to find its greatest power not by itself but in some kind of combination with its opposite. Our consciousness of these two dimensions in which the literary object extends itself, however, seems to me to be made clearer by the enquiry I have been pursuing.

Surely any help which we can gain, from this enquiry or any other, towards understanding the essential nature of literary achievement, and of the limits within which it can vary as it responds to the potentialities of the author's experience or the place open to it in his society—surely any such help is specially valuable at the present time. I do not say this for any of the stock reasons, but for one which is peculiarly connected with the theme of these lectures. It is, that this widening of the horizon which I have been studying must now come to an end. There has been talk of the imaginary museum of literature, from many different cultures and periods, now lying open for the first time before the poet. It seems to me, on the contrary, that we are entering the very period in which, as a truly creative potential, it will close. It will close because over four centuries we in Western Europe and America have opened up, to our literary consciousness, one after another of the major literatures and major cultures of the planet. No doubt there are gaps still to fill. I do not myself find, for example, that the marvellous clarity and purity of vision which instantly strikes me when I open the Vedic hymns (mediocre as most translations are), has ever exercised its due influence on English writing. But filling a gap is one thing, and discovering the new world of a major civilization is another. We have reached in our literary culture the point reached by the geographical explorer some time ago. Peru and Cathay, the wealth of Ormuz and of Ind, had become known to him, and nothing remained but an ever more un-inviting series of South Poles—they open up now, an infinity of spectacular tedium, before the space explorer of today or the future. One way in which this radical change may be very clearly seen is this. With Percy, with Jones, with Pound's translations from the Nō drama or later from the Chinese Classic Anthology, the prize was the *central corpus* of work in an exotic cul-ture. It was some masterpiece, or group of masterpieces, from the whole historical run of an exotic literature. Nowadays the most popular kind of contact is rather with a mere contemporary *avant garde*—in the West Indies, Australia, West Africa, wherever it may be. I do not condemn this in any way. It is clearly in the image of our time and our pre-occupation everywhere with the topical. But it is another kind of thing; and by definition it cannot have an impact of the same magnitude. Perhaps I exaggerated when I said that the widening of the horizon, in my sense, had now come to an end. Perhaps there are enough discoveries to make to last us for another decade or so, another several decades. But, inescapably, the end of that process, and of that kind of stimulus, is in sight. The process of exploration that began in the Renaissance with our own native past and our own western classics, and then opened its horizons wider and wider, is certainly near the limit of its range; and when, in a sense—only in a sense—the whole literature of the planet, over its history, has finally ceased to have for us the appearance of an unexplored and virgin forest, and has become, though alien, a familiar garden—well, by then, how shall we cultivate our own and private garden?

NOTES

I

page	note	
3	1	'The Oral Diffusion of the Arthurian Legend', *Arthurian Literature in the Middle Ages*, ed. R. S. Loomis (1959), pp. 52–63.
3	2	Nennius, Chaps. X and LVI, Gildas, *De Excidio Britanniae*, Chap 26; discussed by K. H. Jackson in Loomis (see note 1), pp. 1–11.
5	3	*The Faerie Queene*, II.10.7.
5	4	*Ibid.*, II.10.6.
5	5	See T. D. Kendrick, *British Antiquity* (1950), p. 129.
6	6	*Polyolbion*, 'Illustrations' to Song VIII.
6	7	*View of the Present State of Ireland*, ed. W. L. Renwick (1934), pp. 51–54; 94–98.
7, 8	8	M. Drayton, *Works*, ed. J. W. Hebel (1961 ed.) Vol. V, p. 84; *Polyolbion*, Song IV, 115; Hebel, Vol. II, pp. 347–9, and cf. the ode *To Sir Henry Goodere*, II, p. 344.
9	9	Kendrick (see note 5), p. 111; p. 115.
9	10	Quoted in D. C. Douglas, *English Scholars* (1951 ed.), p. 53.
10	11	J. G. A. Pocock, *The Ancient Constitution and the Feudal Law* (1957).
10	12	Kendrick, p. 101.
11, 12	13	Douglas, p. 53; pp. 81 ff.
13	14	Quoted by S. Kliger, 'The Neo-Classical View of Old English Poetry', *Journal of English and Germanic Philology*, 1950, pp. 516ff.

14 15 See S. Kliger, 'The Goths in England'; *Modern Philology*, Vol 43 (1945–6), p. 107.

15 16 Paul Henri Mallet, *Northern Antiquities*, Bishop Percy's translation (1770), Vol. I, Chap. 8.

15,16 17 *Northern Antiquities*, I. Percy's note, pp. 170–1; and 173.

16 18 See E. Seaton, *England and Scandinavia in the Seventeenth Century* (1935).

16 19 *Works*, ed. G. Keynes (1964 ed.), Vol. I, p. 147.

17 20 Seaton, p. 226.

17 21 See Pope's note to *The Temple of Fame*, II 119ff.

18 22 *Works* (1754 ed.), Vol. II, pp. 280,338.

19 23 C. H. Herford, *Norse Myth in English Poetry* (1918), p. 9.

20 24 See F. E. Farley, *Scandinavian Influences on the English Romantic Movement* (1905), p. 58 and note.

20 25 Amos Cottle, *Saemund's Edda* (1797). Cottle also repeats, apparently from Percy's translation of Mallet, the idea of the 'equal plan of life which was the peculiar characteristic of all the Gothic tribes'.

22 26 Toland, *Critical History* . . . (London n.d.) Vol. I, pp. 26–27; quoted by Kliger.

22 27 Toland, pp. 47–48.

22 28 M. Martin, *Description of the Western Isles of Scotland* (2nd ed., 1716), p. 9.

24 29 W. J. Hughes, *Wales and the Welsh in English Literature* (1917), p. 70.

25 30 Arnold used Blackwell's translation: see *The Poems of Matthew Arnold*, ed. K. Allott (1965), p. 351.

26 31 *Od.*, XI.38; *Geo.* IV, 476; *Aen.*VI,307; *Inferno*, IV.30.

27 32 *Sigurd the Volsung* (1896 ed.), p. 265 ('Of the mighty grief of Gudrun' etc.); E. Magnusson and W. Morris, *The Story of the Volsungs and Nibelungs*, Chap. 31.

II

32 33 Kendrick, p. 107.

32 34 J. Speed, *History of Great Britain* (1611), Chap. III, para. 4.

32 35 See Farley (note 24), pp. 196–8.

32 36 *Oriental Collections*, ed. Sir William Ouseley (1797), Vol. I, pp. 242–4; II, pp. 1–20.

33	37	*Asiatic Researches* (the *Proceedings* of the Asiatic Society, Bengal, 1791 . . .), Vol. II, pp. 65, 57; see also Granville Penn, 'On the Common Origination of Mankind': *Oriental Collections*, II, p. 65.
35	38	Discussed in H. Javadi-Tabrizi, *The Idea of Persia and Persian Influence on English Literature . . .*, unpublished Ph.D. dissertation, Cambridge University Library, 1965.
36	39	*Iliad*, III.1–4; *Aen.* X.265–6; *Inf.* V.46–48.
36	40	*Sohrab and Rustum*, 450–2; *Iliad*, XXII.25–32.
36	41	*Iliad*, XVII.426ff.
42	42	Clara Reeve, *The Progress of Romance* (1785 ed.), pp. 107–36; Miss Reeve cites Davies' book, and quotes from it, in her Preface (pp. 13–14).
45	43	Noted in Martha P. Conant, *The Oriental Tale in England* (1908), p. 27.
45	44	Collins, *Poetical Works . . . with Observations . . . by J. Langhorne* (1776), p. 113.
46	45	*Asiatic Researches*, III. p. 165.
46	46	Chalmers, *English Poets*, Vol. XVIII (1810 ed.), p. 504.
47	47	Chalmers, p. 503.
47	48	*Oriental Collections*, II. pp. 50–1.
49	49	*Childe Harold*, II. liii–lxvi.
54	50	Chalmers, p. 502. R. M. Hewitt, 'Harmonious Jones' (*Essays and Studies*, 1942) states that Jones was the first Englishman truly to admire Arabic poetry.
55	51	John Pinkerton, *Collections of Voyages and Travels* (1808 ed.), Vol. X, pp. 79, 85.
55	52	Pinkerton, p. 85. Alexander Dow, *History of Hindustan* (1768), Vol. III, pp. 9–10, contrasts the free democratic Arab with the 'violent aristocracy' and despotism of the Tartars.
55	53	Pinkerton, p. 143.

III

| 61 | 54 | Dow, Vol. I, pp. xxi–lxix. |
| 62 | 55 | Edna Osborne, *Oriental Diction and Theme in English Verse, 1740–1800* (Kansas Studies, 1916), p. 88. |

65 56 Chambers: *Hymn to Narayena*, p. 485; *Hymn to Camdeo*, p. 473.

67 57 Arian, *Alexander*, VII. i.

68 58 *Archeologia Philosophiae* (1692 ed.), pp. 352–8.

68 59 Quoted in H. Weber, *Tales of the East* (1812), Vol. I, p. viii. Cf. the reference to the 'simplicity of thought and language' of the Brahmins: Vol. II, p. 537.

69 60 Weber, Vol. I, p. xiii.

70 61 See P. Naravutty, 'William Blake and Hindu Creation Myth', in *The Divine Vision*, ed. V. de Sola Pinto (1957), p. 163. Burnet noted that the Brahmins 'retain the doctrine of the *ovum mundanum*, comparing the world to an egg as did the Ancients both Greek and barbarian'. (*Arch. Phil.*, 1726 transl. *Appendix*, p. 7).

72 61a H. W. Piper, *The Active Universe* (1962), p. 155ff.

74 62 T. H. Griffith, *Specimens of Old Indian Poetry* (1852), p. vii.

77 63 The most recent translation of these poems is by Professor A. J. Arberry, *The Seven Odes* (1957).

77 64 Chalmers (see note 46), p. 504.

78 65 See M. E. de Meester, *Oriental Influences on English Literature in the Nineteenth Century* (1915), pp. 52–4; and Koeppel, *Englische Studien*, Vol. 28 (1900), p. 400ff.

79 66 This poem is briefly discussed, from another standpoint, in Osborne (see note 55), p. 18.

81 67 P. E. More, *The Drift of Romanticism* (1913), pp. 21–22.

82 68 C. R. Lanman, 'Hindu Law and Custom as to Gifts'; *Kittredge Anniversary Papers* (Boston, 1913), pp. 1–13.

IV

85 69 Conant (see note 43), p. 143ff., 184ff.

87 70 Vol. II, p. 158ff.

87 71 Vol. II, p. 196ff.

88 72 E. Arnold, *Japonica* (1892), pp. 117–18.

89 73 Chamberlain, pp. 24–25; Aston, p. 203; Lloyd, *Transactions* of the Asiatic Society of Japan, Vol. 38 (October 1910), pp. 128–31.

89 74 Osman Edwards, *Japanese Plays and Playfellows* (1901), pp. 57, 58.

90 75 Marie Stopes, *Plays of Old Japan* (1913), p. 4.

92 76 Stopes, pp. 20–21; Yeats, *Essays and Introductions* (1961 ed.), pp. 155–6.

95 77 Worringer, *Abstraction and Empathy* (M. Bullock's translation, 1953), p. 133.

99 78 Yeats, *Collected Plays* (1950 ed.), pp. 688–9; *Nō or Accomplishment*, p. 141.

99 79 *The Poems of Egan O'Rahilly*, ed. Rev. P. S. Dineen (Irish Texts Society, 1900), p. 165.

100 80 *The Hidden Ireland* (2nd ed., 1925), p. 229.

100 81 See Jon Stallworthy, *Between the Lines: Yeats's Poetry in the Making* (1963), Chapter V.

101 82 Dineen, pp. 67–87.

102 83 Douglas Hyde, *Songs Ascribed to Raftery* (1903), p. 49. I have discussed these matters more fully in *Yeats and the Penal Age* (B.B.C. Third Programme, 1 August 1965; subsequently printed in *The Critical Quarterly*, Spring 1966).

102 84 *The Common Muse* (1957), p. 26.

104 85 *Edinburgh Review*, Vol. 29 (November 1817), p. 2; quoted in Osborne (see note 54), p. 141.

106 86 Marcelle A. Hincks, 'The Art of Dancing in Japan': *Fortnightly Review*, July 1906, p. 85ff; see especially p. 91.